Winter
Passages

Winter Passages

Reflections on Theatre and Society

Robert Brustein

Transaction Publishers
New Brunswick (U.S.A.) and London (U.K.)

This book is printed on acid-free paper that meets the American National Standard for Permanence of Paper for Printed Library Materials.

Library of Congress Catalog Number: 2014005886
ISBN: 978-1-4128-5473-3
Printed in the United States of America

Library of Congress Cataloging-in-Publication Data

Brustein, Robert Sanford, 1927-
Winter passages : reflections on theatre and society / by Robert Brustein.
    pages cm
  ISBN 978-1-4128-5473-3
  1. Theater and society. I. Title.
    PN2051.B79 2015
    792--dc23

2014005886

Contents

Acknowledgments

The essays on Thornton Wilder, Weill and Lenya, and China were written for *The New York Review*. *More Masterpieces* in the *Performing Arts Journal*. *Puttin' on the Spritz* was commissioned for Mel Brooks's DVD collection. *The Like Generation* and *Return of the Booboisie* appeared in *The Huffington Post*. *The Institution as a Work of Art* was a speech to a business group.

All of the pieces on playwrights were written as introductions for *Playwrights in an Hour*, as commissioned by Smith and Krause—the one exception being my essay on Christopher Durang, which was commissioned by *Lincoln Center* magazine.

Most of the tributes and elegies were written on the occasion of prizes and memorials at the ART, though the speech on Robert Woodruff was given for the Theatre for a New Audience, and the essay on Philip Roth appeared in the *Huffington Post*. My thanks to all those periodicals and institutions for permission to reprint.

I have also been deeply fortunate in my editors, for their vigilance in wiping egg off my face—Robert Silvers at *The New York Review of Books*; Marisa Smith at Smith and Krause; John Guare at *Lincoln Center Theatre Magazine*; and, of course, my chief editor at home, Doreen Beinart; and Jennifer Nippins of Transaction Publishers.

Introduction:
The Past is Prologue

For many educated people in America the postmillennial years have seemed like one long winter of discontent, and we have yet to see much sign of glorious summer. Among those feeling more than their customary quota of gloom I count myself, admittedly a famously disgruntled commentator. (My earliest reviews were collected in 1965 under the title of *Seasons of Discontent*.)

In those years, I was feeling cranky over the small number of good plays on the American stage. Today, I am more depressed by our political-cultural system itself. The general reasons for this are discussed, sometimes obliquely, in the first section of this book, "Cultural Passages." But let me try to sketch out in this introduction some of the reasons for my darker mood.

I think the source of the problem is that we no longer have a strong social-economic system, such as Marxism or socialism, to modify human selfishness or curtail human greed, and organized religion doesn't seem to be doing much to improve human character either (though the early days of Pope Francis's papacy are proving promising). The result is evident today in virtually every social endeavor, including the theatre.

Admittedly, this represents a reversion to an old condition. Although world theatre originated in ritual rather than commerce and was thereafter kept alive through a combination of patronage and ticket sales, in the United States theatre began as a fundamentally profit-oriented entertainment, like the circus, until the late twentieth century, when a number of alternative partially-subsidized institutions grew up to challenge the commercial system in every major city. Represented by the resident theatre movement and the avant-garde, these alternative stages constituted a growing high culture in theatre to match that in American fine arts, music, opera, and ballet, creating a healthy tension between the "art theatre" and the "money theatre," to quote Todd London's indispensable description of the divergent poles of our theatre culture. The "art theatre" survived, in its purest form, for the last fifty years of the twentieth century. Now the two antagonists seem to have settled their argument and merged as most of these alternative expressions are being sucked into the yawning gullet of corporate America.

And it's not just theatres. The closing down of book shops; the shrinking of audiences for all performance venues, especially opera and ballet; the loss of readership for, and consequent dumbing down of, newspapers and magazines with any serious content; and the timidity of publishing houses—indeed, almost every available cultural (and educational) form of activity—seem to be signaling the end of an adventurous alternative. Even terms like "highbrow" and "intellectual" are becoming recherché or obsolete as the institutions, publications, and structures that attracted such rarefied beings in the past are going out of business or being absorbed into the Internet.

As for the commercialization of serious theatres, it began with the loss of a dependable source of subsidized support, along with the dwindling in size of adventurous audiences. This development motivated some of the nonprofit companies to begin popularizing their work in a manner almost indistinguishable from Broadway, with its traditional pattern of following rather than leading public taste. The practical reason given for this populist move in the resident theatre was to increase income. But a high-minded political motive was being forwarded, too, which was to increase the size of audiences by avoiding the taint of "elitism"—perhaps the most invidious term ever invented to discourage leadership in the arts. It was Chekhov who said, "You must bring the people up to Gogol, not Gogol down to the people." Imagine how that admonition would be received today! First the National Endowment for the Arts, feeble enough to start with, sustained serious body blows from a Congress fearful of artistic expression as a whole. Then, foundations, corporations, and individual donors grew a great deal more capricious in their giving habits. And finally, political correctness in the university and elsewhere, with its imposition of multicultural quotas and its substitution of "critical theory" for textual analysis, is making sure that genuine quality (or "elitism") would no longer be the primary criterion for creation. Instead of debates over the aesthetic of an artist or the meaning of a particular work of art, attention is being shifted to complaints about the scarcity of gay plays or the number of women playwrights or whether "black" actors should perform in "white" parts or whether "white" directors should stage "black" theatre or whether "white" actors should be allowed to play "Latinos" and all the other variations on these sexual, gendered, racial, and ethnic determinants.

True, there have almost always been restraints of some kind, usually moral or religious, on freedom of expression in the theatre. Shakespeare and his contemporaries, for example, were forced to cast "squeaking boys" in female parts because the Church objected to women performing on a public stage. (English Puritans, on the other hand, citing biblical proscriptions on cross-dressing, would shut down spoken theatre entirely in 1642, permitting—does this sound familiar?—only musical production on stage.) Elizabethan and Jacobean playwrights, like many writers functioning under watchdog agencies, usually found some strategy with which to evade government restraints. But imagine if the Greeks or Shakespeare's company at the Globe or Molière's Comédie-Francaise or Stanislavski's Moscow Art Theatre or Britain's Royal Shakespeare Company and National Theatre had been forced to abide by multicultural dictates—or if, like today, artistic people were pouring their valuable creative energies into dancing around cultural obstacles. We would have inherited a very different theatre tradition.

The celebrated European companies, though often functioning under repressive regimes, were usually able to operate without being seriously muffled, while our democracy, with its insistence on equality in all things except where it really matters—income and status and education—seems willing to jettison artistic standards in return for an appearance of equal opportunity.

As a political animal myself, I have fought for equal opportunity all my life, so I am hardly arguing that the theatre should close itself off from social change. I am simply arguing that artists be judged, if I may paraphrase Martin Luther King, on the quality of their talent rather than the color of their skin—or their gender and ethnicity. When political and sociological inhibitions begin to invade the precincts of art, and shape its direction, then our culture begins to resemble those under totalitarian regimes, though controlled less by autocratic decree than by self-censorship and punitive funding decisions.

The background for all of this is largely political. As a result of the election and reelection of President Obama—and the racist recoil against the existence of a black chief executive—our democratic system has reached one of the lowest points in its history. The current Congress has been described as dysfunctional. It would be more accurately characterized as nonfunctional, even antifunctional, with the Tea Party composed not of Boston revolutionaries but of red state anarchists bent on sabotaging our whole system of government.

In a society so dedicated to profit and acquisition, even such usually dependable and disinterested institutions as the university are growing indistinguishable in purpose from the corporate world. The number of liberal arts majors has fallen precipitously. Many English departments no longer even require a Shakespeare course, and Chemistry departments are often encouraged, even in some of the most prestigious institutions of higher learning, to develop profitable products for drug companies. Meanwhile, most lower schools are no longer requiring arts education, since the first person to go when money is short is the music teacher, and the next generation is growing up, bald faced, untutored, and without any exposure to the best things that have been thought and written. In place of a hunger for aesthetic or spiritual nourishment, we have violent scenes of greedy acquisition—like those wild mobs assaulting each other in the act of grabbing Black Friday bargains at Walmarts. A needy class side by side with a greedy class produces selfishness and resentment, two of the basest human qualities.

As a result, there are very few places to look for solace for our current cultural problems. One of them is among the talents of our artists, a number of whom I have chosen to celebrate in the second and third sections of the book, "Playwright Passages" and "Commemorative Passages." For, as Philip Roth has noted, if politics generalizes and art particularizes, then today we desperately need to look into the hearts of individuals, not unruly multitudes. Just as great works of art have the capacity to transform our souls and even, occasionally, make us better beings, so such gifted artists, regardless of their personal characteristics (often as fallible as ours), still have the capacity to sustain and rehabilitate our faith in humankind. I am more and more coming to believe that they are among the few hopes remaining for respite from an increasingly savage economic and social system.

1

Cultural Passages

The Institution as a Work of Art

There has always been a trace of suspicion, a hint of opposition, a touch of wariness between business and the arts, despite their often natural affinities. No one can deny that nonprofit institutions are financially dependent, to a greater or lesser degree, on the kindness of strangers in the corporate world. Who would have enjoyed a Metropolitan Opera House broadcast, for example, without the support of the oil companies or listened to the New York Philharmonic on radio without MetLife? It is also true that business people have traditionally made up a large, if sometimes reluctant, proportion of arts audiences. (Think of the stereotype of the tired businessman, snoring through a play or a concert, oblivious to his wife's embarrassed efforts to nudge him awake.)

But considering their differing purposes, the artist and the businessman would seem to be occupying different worlds. The one is dedicated to advancing the imagination, the other to increasing profit. The one is devoted to satisfying audiences with pleasing objects, the other to satisfying shareholders with prosperous balance sheets. Indeed, one American tradition finds the poet and the businessman to be in eternal opposition, glaring at one another across an unbreachable chasm. This was certainly the popular Bohemian assumption of the 1920s, as well as the repeated subject of most of the plays of Eugene O'Neill, especially *The Great God Brown*.

As the son of a wool merchant and as one who has led theatre institutions for over forty years, however, I have come to believe that the artist and the businessman might have a lot more in common than is commonly assumed. Indeed, they might even be blood relations. John Adams once said that he was a politician so that his son could be a businessman so that *his* son could be an artist. Adams was talking about parental subsidy, of course—about American capital creating the kind of financial conditions fertile for the arts. That Utopian condition has obviously not yet materialized here, as it has in Europe and Asia. But rather than assail you about America's failed responsibilities to the arts—I would be happy to do this on another occasion—let me frame this in a more positive way, as a future objective. For I believe that, in their best manifestations, business and the arts are indeed capable of sharing the same blood lines, objectives, and ideals. To illustrate this, let me run a controversial thought by you, to wit, that any company or corporation, whether artistic or commercial, is in a position to achieve the conditions of a work of art. In other words, I am suggesting that any human institution, whether for profit or not for profit, however subject to human error, greed, or power drives, can aspire toward an ideal social condition.

Stated so baldly, this may sound absurd, and I wouldn't be surprised to hear a few catcalls issuing both from the institutionalists and the anti-institutionalists alike. Many creative artists like to think of themselves as being in revolt against organized society, organized religion, and even organized art. Such people are likely to believe that institutions are anti-individualistic, if not antihuman, by their very nature and that the best condition for creating lasting work is to be alone with a pencil and pad in a shuttered room or with a brush and easel in a sunlit atelier. I know one stage director, and a fine one, who has declared it his mission to kill every theatre he works in by directing productions designed to send the audience screaming out of the theatre. Peter Handke once wrote a play called *Offending the Audience*. That is the objective of not a few creative artists. Why? If pressed, some might claim that rather than being a contribution to social harmony, their own work was an effort to reject the world botched up by God and offer a better version.

As for practical businessmen, they tend to look on creative people as impossible dreamers, incapable of managing their own bank accounts much less the conduct of society. Give the artist an allowance and, like a wayward teenager, he will soon waste it on drink like F. Scott Fitzgerald or drugs like Allen Ginsberg or trips to Tahiti like Paul Gauguin and then hold out his hand for more. How can the artist pontificate about how to run a business when he can't even manage his own laundry? That is why the artistic personnel of theatres, operas, symphonies, and dance companies have traditionally been reinforced with the equivalent of hardheaded business managers, namely executive directors and treasurers and marketers and development officers, whose job security depends not on laissez-faire free spending but rather on balancing their institution's income and expense ledgers and keeping it from going belly up. Especially during a time when the arts are gasping for financial breath, why should anyone be asked to reexamine the structures in which they work for any reason other than to generate a lot more capital for the organization?

My answer is that just as our Founding Fathers, who even encouraged an occasional revolution from time to time, expected the Constitution to be continually amended in order to adopt to the changing conditions of American society, so it is essential that the smaller American social units continually revise their own constitutions in order to avoid freezing into conventionality and rigidity and indifference. I would go even further. True leadership in business and the arts requires not that they keep up with the society in which they function but rather that they keep ahead of it, advancing and improving rather than reflecting its more wayward or careless values. Sometimes this means inventing alternatives to the current models—models that point toward a more ideal system. This system is what I am calling the institution as a work of art. To illustrate the idea better, let me offer you some examples from my personal experience.

I have been involved now with the founding of four different theatre organizations, two of which are still in existence—the Yale Repertory Theatre, which I led for thirteen years, and the American Repertory Theatre for almost two and a half decades. Although I no longer run either, both continue to function effectively under different artistic directors. And although it is arguable whether theatres should remain faithful to their founding principles, the process of change has inevitably pulled both in different directions. Those concepts and those changes may help illustrate my initial point.

I created the Yale Repertory Theatre at Yale University in 1966 after President Kingman Brewster invited me to become the Dean of the School of Drama. As one who had spent a hapless year at this school in the late forties before leaving in some disgruntlement, I was reluctant at first to accept his offer. Following its early glory days in the late twenties and thirties under George Pierce Baker, the Harvard English Professor of Playwriting who founded it, the Yale School of Drama had grown stodgy and tired. It was turning out teachers rather than theatre professionals. And it was being run like a military academy in a manner that pinched the creative spirit and squelched the imagination. The Drama School, in other words, had lost a lot of its original drive and purpose. Baker had been the mentor of Eugene O'Neill, Philip Barry, Sidney Howard, among others—playwrights who were trying to revolutionize the commercial theatre system with a whole new theatrical vision and spirit. By the beginning of the sixties, the Yale School of Drama was mostly turning out people who, if they even remained in the professional theatre at all rather than gravitating toward university theatre departments, were mostly content with the tired conventions of Broadway.

I told Brewster that I could not accept the job unless I was allowed to make profound alterations in the structure and purpose of the school. The president barely flinched at my presumptuous demand. He was himself dissatisfied with the existing system and was willing to give me considerable latitude in changing it. For one thing, I wanted to replace some of the existing tenured faculty, most of whom had been my teachers twenty years earlier, with professionals from the field. Secondly, I wanted to get rid of tenure. I needed practitioners not theoreticians, and I needed people more interested in keeping up with developments in the field than guarding their tenured security.

As someone who was professing a humane artistic environment, my first request on the face of it would seem to have been a rather heartless one. But my new broom did not actually affect anybody's livelihood. By luck, most of these tenured teachers were nearing retirement anyway, and, since Yale's was a three-year program, I was able to keep most of them on to guide the graduating class they had originally admitted, with the first and second year classes being exposed to the incoming faculty. Brewster managed to accommodate my need for the additional salaries by immediately promoting a $340,000 grant from the Rockefeller Foundation for seven new positions. Through a combination of part-time slots and positions paid for partly by our professional company, we managed to increase those seven positions to twenty-one without spending a single extra dollar.

Brewster responded positively to my second request as well, which was to form a nonprofit professional theatre company as an adjunct to the school. But for this new venture, he added, I would have to raise the funds myself. As a previously-tenured faculty member at Columbia, I had never raised a penny in my life, but it was clear that this pristine condition was about to change. I soon raised the wherewithal through another Rockefeller grant of $300,000 plus generous gifts from individuals, including $50,000 from Paul Newman before he founded Newman's Own. And it didn't hurt that some of the actors, directors, and designers we attracted were being partially paid by Yale as teachers. Why did I need a professional theatre company when I was running a professional school? My archetype was the Old Vic Theatre and the Old Vic School in London—not to mention Stanislavski's Moscow Art Theatre and School. I wanted a theatre company that would serve as a training ground, a theatrical model, and an area of future employment for my drama students. I thought that the university, with its selfless devotion to learning and ideas, could be a perfect place to develop a new kind of theatre institution, one that served not just as a conduit to the commercial theatre but as an alternative to it. And with attention growing in the press over something new that was happening at Yale, I was able to attract a large number of fine professionals, serving both as teachers and as theatre artists, who had already distinguished themselves in the American theatre. Some, like Stella Adler and Bobby Lewis, had trained in the Group Theatre, one of the country's most successful efforts to develop a serious theatre art. Others, like Joe Chaikin, Andre Gregory, Joe Papp, Bernard Gersten,

Richard Gilman, Alvin Epstein, Arnold Weinstein, and Gordon Rogoff, came from the world of off-Broadway or, in the case of Robert Lowell, Joe Heller, and Jerzy Kosiński, from the world of literature. Still others, like Jonathan Miller and Kenneth Haigh and Irene Worth, came from England, which already had a distinguished subsidized theatre with much to teach us about ours.

My businessman father, a wool jobber, always had a dream about what he called a "vertical combination." He wanted not only to sell the carded and combed wool product, but to dye it and spin it as well, in order to manufacture sweaters. I had a similar dream, but not about bringing wool yarn from the backs of the sheep to the backs of the customers. I wanted to take young student actors, directors, playwrights, designers, literary directors, and technicians through a process of initiation and training to a process of full professional activity. Thus, they would not only be able to practice their profession but perhaps teach it to the next generation as well, as they themselves had been taught by their older professional colleagues. My model was the medical school where future doctors were being trained under the supervision of practicing physicians and surgeons and then serving as interns and later as residents in a teaching hospital.

Of course we knew that it was unrealistic to expect all of our students to devote themselves continuously to the modest conditions of nonprofit theatres. We were aware that a large number would inevitably be seeking more lucrative careers on Broadway, in Hollywood, and in television. Although there was always a certain degree of monasticism in our training, and although we lectured our students continually about the necessity "to love the art in themselves rather than themselves in art," as Stanislavsky put it, they were free upon graduation to go wherever they wanted in pursuit of their careers. On the other hand, we hoped that the atmosphere of the place would translate itself into a lifelong devotion to the theatre. And most of our students, heeding that call, remained loyal to the stage, even those who later achieved great celebrity and stardom in other media. The actors Meryl Streep, Henry Winkler, Ken Howard, Jill Eikenberry, Sigourney Weaver, Mark Linn-Baker, James Naughton, and Tony Shalhoub; the playwrights Christopher Durang, Ted Tally, Albert Innaurato, David Epstein, and Wendy Wasserstein; and the comedian Lewis Black are only a few among a long list of our successful graduates.

Actually, the greatest competition during these early years, which were also the years of Vietnam, was not from the commercial stage but from the political theatre. Their passions inflamed by what was perceived to be an unjust and unnecessary conflict, not much different from Iraq today, and by a few presidents who couldn't bring themselves to tell the truth about it, our students were often on the streets of New Haven or marching in Washington when they should have been thinking about voice classes or acting projects. This was also the time of May Day at Yale, when the trial of Black Panther Bobby Seale for allegedly ordering the murder of a black informer was threatening to bring down explosive radical wrath upon the entire university. Often, I would find students violating the sacred half-hour rule, when you have to be in your dressing room thirty minutes before curtain time, because they were standing in front of the theatre with placards screaming "Free Bobby Seale."

Brewster tried to preserve his endangered university, and demonstrate the civilized nature of a liberal arts institution, by inviting the outside protesters inside the walls of Yale and suspending all academic activities so we could discuss the plight of the Panthers. I respected his decision. Was it not his way of trying to turn the university into a work of art? But I questioned it as a violation of the principles of free scholarship, free art, and free expression, a kind of intellectual collapse under ideological pressure, so I refused to shut down either the theatre or the school. Brewster saved the university but alienated a lot of Old Blue alumni, becoming one of Spiro Agnew's "nattering nabobs of negativism." I saved my principles but enraged a lot of radicals. There were even threats against my life and a bullet through my neighbor's window, obviously meant for mine. Nobody emerged a winner.

But although the political climate had considerably slowed down the process, by the end of my thirteen years at Yale we had pretty much accomplished our purpose, which was to find some way to balance the needs of the individual against the demands of the institution, and satisfy them both. Most artists pursue their profession in solitude. Theatre artists, like those in corporate life, must work in collaboration with each other. This means the artistic ego has to find a way to express itself without violating the rights and needs of the host institution. Likewise, the institution has to find a way to function without trampling on the rights and needs of the artistic ego. Isn't that how the larger society ought to function? And isn't that where the larger society almost inevitably fails us to one degree or other? The totalitarian model insists on total subordination of the individual to the state. The anarchist model exalts the individual over the social organism, rejecting any laws that infringe on the rights of human freedom. Somewhere between these two extremes is a model that satisfies the shared needs of the community while letting the individual flower and develop.

The purpose of a humane theatre company—I believe it should be the goal of any kind of company—is to stimulate the artistic juices of its membership in order to encourage continuous creative growth. This means that season productions must be chosen not just to satisfy audiences, but also to advance the talents of the artists. Actors, for example, should have the opportunity to play a great variety of roles, unrestricted by their age group or temperament. Great actors do not continually recreate aspects of their own personality, but rather continually transform themselves into the lives of others. This is called character acting or "transformation" and it is the very opposite of the kind of personality acting you often see being practiced by stars in the movies, on television, and on the commercial stage. True transformation invites a kind of anonymity and does not often stimulate fan clubs, though Meryl Streep, for one, managed the difficult feat of becoming both a star and a character actress. Meryl's first professional appearance when still a student at the Drama School took place on the stage of the Yale Repertory Theatre playing an ancient crone named Constance Garnett in a satiric play called *The Idiots Karamazov*. She was imprisoned in a wheelchair, with a grey wig over her blond tresses, her eyes oozing plum tree gum, her aquiline nose turned into a witch's beak with a wart on it. It was the triumph of talent over vanity. She was already proving herself a great transforming artist.

And shouldn't that be a crucial goal of the corporate world as well, to uncover strengths in an employee that are not immediately apparent? This means that managers should try to end typecasting as well. Employees should have the opportunity to fill any job they are qualified for, the only true criterion being not age or race or sex or seniority or being one of the boss's cronies, but simply having the talent and capacity to perform that job well. I am aware that there have been many businesses that, in their sensitivity to their employees and the world around them, have approached being a work of art. Ben and Jerry's, for example, until it was swallowed up in a corporate buyout, was extraordinarily sensitive to the environment. Stride Rite, in Massachusetts, was one of the first Boston businesses to provide day care for its female employees. Even the much maligned Walmart, often correctly accused of violating labor laws, is now making more of an effort to make its employees feel included in the process. This has not been the norm in our world of glass ceilings and tenure tracks and job categories and Pac-Man-like corporate takeovers. But anyone interested in forming a new business or a new arts organization or even a new political administration must have somewhere in mind, either consciously or unconsciously, the desire to succeed where others often fail, namely in creating an alternative system dedicated to the happiness and fulfillment of all its members, where the best are allowed and encouraged to rise to the top.

That alternative is what I mean by the institution as a work of art. Is it achievable? Of course not. At least not consistently, and perhaps only in rare instances, but we perceive it often enough to make it an ideal toward which to strive. In the arts, ironically, it is rarely a democratic model, because the arts are hierarchical, created by a single, hopefully gifted individual and then led by a strong figure at the top, comparable to a chief executive officer of a corporation. I am thinking of artists like the late Ingmar Bergman and his Stockholm Royal Dramatic Theatre or Ivo Von Hove and his Toneelgroep in Amsterdam, the undisputed leaders and arbiters of everything that appears on stage.

There have been occasionally been collectives in the theatre, libertarian in nature, like The Living Theatre of the 1960s and 70s, which wandered through the land like gypsies, involving their audiences in group gropes and pseudo-orgies on stage. But even that sort of freedom is a mirage. Julian Beck and Judith Malina, the leaders of The Living Theatre, exercised a control over their followers and audiences that was almost dictatorial. I remember one evening during an appearance at Yale, when a woman student went up to the microphone to protest their procedures and was hustled off the stage by actors pretending to fondle and embrace her. This was suppression masquerading as love. In a similar way, Peter Brook's International Centre for Theatre Research in Paris, a commune of international theatre artists, while supposedly honoring the creative impulses of people from all over the world, is informed by the powerful vision of its brilliant but highly autocratic leader, who is sometimes accused of applying the theatrical version of colonialism.

However responsive to the needs of the group, one person ultimately has to make the decisions in the creative process. But sometimes, paradoxically, the most apparently dictatorial directors turn out to be the most communal and cooperative. The great theatre visionary, Robert Wilson, who exercises authority over every aspect of his productions, not just the staging but the text, lighting, scene design, costumes, production, and even fundraising, who directs his actors with what seems like metronomic precision, is at the same time one of the most collaborative of artists, allowing the utmost freedom within the strict confines of his design. This is why he can work so well with such strong-minded artists as Philip Glass, Tom Waits, Jesse Norman, Heiner Müller, Isabelle Huppert, and Lucinda Childs. (May I include our theatre and myself? We did five of his productions at the American Repertory Theatre, including my own adaptation of Ibsen's *When We Dead Awaken.*)

There are also some artists, as I am sure there are some business leaders and managers, who try to squelch any effort that departs from their own single-minded ideas. Lord Acton has told us that if power corrupts, absolute power corrupts absolutely. And this corruption can lead to the same danger that threatens every hierarchical organization, namely an abuse of power by those at the top who try to prevent the young and gifted from rising. Solness, the architect hero of Ibsen's *The Master Builder* was a prime example of these, terrified of the "younger generation," running a firm in which his assistants were treated like slaves. So is the architect hero of Ayn Rand's *The Fountainhead*, who would rather blow up his building than compromise its aesthetic. Many plays of the twenties, notably Elmer Rice's *The Adding Machine* and Sophie Treadwell's *Machinal*, imagine a business climate in which the employees toil at their desks like worker ants, supervised by a tyrant who barks orders at them like an unfeeling drill sergeant. I am reminded of an old movie called *The Seventh Veil*, in which the actress, Ann Todd, played a pianist forced by her tyrannical guardian, played by James Mason, to practice her instrument six hours a day without a stop. Naturally, she falls madly in love with him.

My experiment with ideal institutions at Yale was ended in 1979 when the new president, A. Bartlett Giamatti, later the Commissioner of Baseball, fired me. As a Yale undergraduate, and later my colleague in the Yale English department, he preferred an older version of Yale Drama School where he had courted his wife, so, just as he was later to suspend Pete Rose for his moral infractions, he fired me for aesthetic infractions. Well, he didn't actually fire me. He just declared my administration to be at an end and appointed my successor, Lloyd Richards. Richards was the excellent dean and artistic director who was the first to bring August Wilson to national attention. But he had entirely different ideas about the place than I did—different ideas even from the president who wanted to return the school to its earlier academic environment. But one of Richards' first actions was to disband the resident company. So rather than watch my company disappear, I brought it to Harvard in 1979—forty people in all, including directors, designers, business managers, and virtually the entire graduating class of Yale Drama School, thus proving that if an institution has any intrinsic strength, it can survive migration, even without an ark.

With all those young people in the company joining the veterans who had been their teachers, I finally had achieved my vertical combination at Yale. But I was not at first allowed to continue it at Harvard. President Derek Bok, though warm and welcoming, could not imagine a drama school at the university when it didn't offer an undergraduate drama major or, for that matter, a single theatre course for credit—that is, until we arrived and introduced twelve of them. George Pierce Baker had left for Yale because of the infertile conditions he experienced at Harvard where courses in theatre had been compared to courses in "butchering meat." Now I was able to take his training idea back where it had started, but it would be five years before we managed to persuade the administration that an Advanced Institute for Theatre Training, as we called it, would not be a blemish on the Harvard escutcheon.

We were allowed our school of drama so long as we did not call it a school—(Harvard liked the word "institute") or offer a degree—or ask Harvard for any money. We agreed to all those conditions, though we later did an end run by importing some Russian teachers and sending our students to Moscow for four months, where they earned Master of Fine Arts degrees from the Moscow Arts Theatre School. Our first productions included some of the more popular items from our New Haven repertory, proving another business truism, which is that if you have a popular product keep it in the market—i.e. "If it ain't broke, don't fix it." One of the great virtues of a permanent company, performing in rotating sequence rather than straight runs, is that, unlike most theatrical situations where the show evaporates the moment it closes, you can keep a presentation alive by storing it in repertory—in the manner of an opera company or a dance company or a symphony orchestra. Thus, with some of our more successful shows—like Molière's *Sganarelle* or the Carlo Gozzi-Andrei Şerban-Julie Taymor *The King Stag* or my own version of Pirandello's *Six Characters in Search of an Author*—we were able to bring them back into repertory from time to time, as well as to tour them at festivals in America, Europe, Israel, and Asia.

Speaking of *Six Characters in Search of an Author*, this production was a perfect example of an institutionally created work of theatre in which every member of the cast was encouraged to make contributions. Pirandello imagines six unfinished dramatic characters entering a theatre during a rehearsal of one of his other plays and asking the actors to complete the parts that the author abandoned. I was responsible for the adaptation—my usual way of cost-cutting royalties at the theatre—and also for the staging when the original director, Andrei Şerban, had a conflict. To increase the contrast between imagined characters and real actors, I decided to have the six characters interrupt a rehearsal of one of our own productions, and, more importantly, to have the actors play their parts under their own names. Thus, instead of Pirandello's Leading Man, Leading Lady, Ingénue, and so forth, rehearsing Pirandello's *The Rules of the Game*, we had characters named Harry (Murphy), Jeremy (Geidt), Karen (MacDonald), Tony (Shalhoub), Tommy (Derrah), etc. rehearsing Gozzi's *King Stag*, the other play in repertory with it. And instead of Pirandello's dialogue in the mouths of the acting company, I had them use their own. The result was a quite chilling collision between illusion and reality, which left the audiences shaken and moved.

The important thing was the participation of the company in the making of the play. Actors, above all theatre workers, often feel constrained by having to speak the playwright's lines, having to obey the director's staging, having to wear the costumer's clothes, and having to perform within the confines of the stage designer's set. The more a director is able to involve them in the process the happier they are. Whether actors are performing in my original plays or in my adaptations of other people's plays, I am always eager to consider their suggestions about how to revise a line or a scene, and I advise every playwright and director to follow that example.

The last actor in the theatrical equation is the audience, so similar to the consumer's relationship to the product. In the theatre, it is not just important to satisfy the customer, it is essential to involve that customer in the process of the play. Particularly in the commercial theatre where people come to see the latest hits rather than follow the progress of a company through a series of plays, too many audience members are made to feel like voyeurs, peeking into the behavior of others between the rising and the falling of the curtain. But since the live theatre is one of the few remaining places where people are permitted to collect into a community, it is essential that the spectator be encouraged to transcend a passive role and become a participant as well.

One obvious way is to have actors breaking through the fourth wall and addressing the audience directly, as Shakespeare often did with his choral speeches, monologues, and soliloquies. Another way is by actually bringing the spectator on stage, as one of our directors did in a production of Henry IV, when audience members were invited to join a banquet with Falstaff, Shallow, and Silence. Another way is to engage audiences in pre- or post-performance discussions, preferably with the playwrights, director, and actors or with specialists in the field of the play. This is an invaluable device, especially if the production is a radical reinterpretation of a beloved classic, because the aims of the theatre can be better explained and discussed and made more manifest through the process of verbal interchange.

How much more intelligent would certain business decisions have been had the consumer been consulted beforehand? We might have been spared the nuisance of those ghastly plastic packages that require shears or a hack saw or a ton of dynamite in order to reach the item enclosed inside. We might have been spared the anguish of waiting in endless lines at airline counters and supermarket checkouts. We might have been spared the frustration of the automated telephone, being passed between press one for English and press two for Español and press three for Sanskrit and then being shunted robotically through sixteen more protocols before reaching an actual human being. We might even have been spared that more troubling tendency to extend the man hours of nonunion workers, especially in financial institutions working on deals, who often don't get home until long after the meat has grown cold and the dessert has turned to mush, required to climb in bed with a sleeping wife, without ever having the chance to say goodnight to the children.

The last issue binding the arts to business is the question of succession. Who will lead the organization after the founding director or the powerful CEO has retired or died? I have experienced this dilemma twice now: once involuntarily at Yale in 1979 and once by choice in 2002 when I retired from my leadership post and participated in the choice of my first successor (Robert Woodruff), though not the second (Diane Paulus). I have also watched this process in a number of theatre institutions that have lost their first generation of artistic leaders. I don't pretend to be any wiser about this question now than when I was a young man.

The instinct most of us shared was to appoint someone who replicated our own qualities and was prepared to protect the legacy. Those of us who liked the cutting edge were attracted to more radical directors; those in the mainstream preferred the tried-and-true. Regardless of whom we chose, all of us, almost without exception, witnessed the dissolution of our permanent acting companies. Joe Papp's first choice at the New York Shakespeare Festival was JoAnne Akalaitis, a director with the avant-garde Mabou Mines, who started off crippled by the *New York Times* arguing strongly against her candidacy and the paper ultimately toppled her from her post after two seasons. She was succeeded by George C. Wolfe, a more popular choice with ties to Broadway. After Adrian Hall at Trinity Rep retired, he was succeeded by Anne Bogart who inflamed the conservative Providence audiences with her experimental productions of Brecht and deconstructed Broadway musicals, including a radical version of *A Christmas Carol*. She was replaced after one season by Oskar Eustis, who later took over at the Public. The succession to Zelda Fichandler at the Arena Stage in Washington went in the opposite direction. Where Zelda had maintained a permanent company of excellent actors performing a modern repertory of American and European classics, Molly Smith opted for a more conventional schedule of Broadway and off-Broadway hits, including the standard version of *A Christmas Carol*.

My own succession at the ART was more complicated. Working closely with then President Rudenstine, we hit on the idea of a troika structure, elevating our managing director to a more executive position where he could exercise more control over the direction of the theatre, hiring the cutting-edge Robert Woodruff as artistic director, and adding our young English-born Oxford-educated dramaturge, Gideon Lester, as associate director, to guard the legacy, to lead the intellectual aspect of the institution, and to perform the kind of schmoozing with board members that Woodruff was reluctant to do.

This troika encountered both notable artistic successes and considerable financial difficulties. With Woodruff being one of those directors who likes to test the limits of his audience, the ART began experiencing a sizeable decline in subscription numbers and box office revenue, which put some strains on our endowment and frightened Harvard's budget people.

Also, I regret to say, the ART pulled out of rotating repertory and only a handful of company members remained. The current ART administration, under Diane Paulus, is proving to be much more populist in its play choices, not to mention its relationship to the Broadway theatre. The question remains whether business will imitate the arts or the arts will begin to follow a commercial model.

Obviously, the arts do not hold the answer to every human problem. It is famously said, in fact, that the arts don't solve problems at all, but, at best, merely present them correctly. On the other hand, the arts have the capacity to satisfy the creative desires and instincts of the people who practice them, and if that goal can be obtained in arts institutions, then there is no reason it cannot be a model for every species of endeavor. The theatre is the only activity I know that calls its product both a "work" and a "play." It is a profession both mischievous and serious, relaxed and intense, lunatic and exalted, individual and communal. These are qualities that all of us were born with and all of us would like to practice into old age. They coalesce in artists and artistic organizations. There is no reason they cannot coalesce in every human institution.

(1999/2014)

More Masterpieces

In 1967, I wrote a controversial essay called "No More Masterpieces," in which, following the French radical theorist Antonin Artaud (*The Theatre and Its Double*) and the Polish critic Jan Kott (*Shakespeare Our Contemporary*), I argued against slavish reproduction of classical works. I agreed that we had reached the end of some cycle in staging these plays, that actor-dominated classics, particularly Shakespeare, were beginning to resemble opera more than theatre, with their sumptuous settings, brocaded costume parades, and warbled arias. I believed that modern directors were now obliged to freshen our thinking about classical writers in the same way that modern playwrights—notably O'Neill, Cocteau, Sartre, and T. S. Eliot—were freely re-envisioning the Greeks.

My hope was for approaches that would revitalize familiar works wrapped in a cocoon of academic reverence or paralyzed by arthritic convention. Theatre, being a material medium, was settling too cozily into ostentatious display, disregarding the poetic core of a text, its thematic purpose and inner meaning. One way to avoid this, I thought, was through metaphorical investigation by an imaginative director, in close collaboration with a visionary designer, into locating the central image of a play through visual icons and a unified style.

This was what Peter Brook was doing, before his years in France, with the Royal Shakespeare Company in revitalized productions of *A Midsummer Night's Dream* (channeling its youthful energies into acrobatics and circus acts) and *King Lear* (translating its vision of old age and death into a bleak visual vocabulary influenced by Beckett). Such productions were making Shakespeare our contemporary through suggestive associations, bringing audiences a fresh appreciation of classics in danger of dying from hardened stage arteries.

There was another modernizing technique already in vogue at the time called "Updating." This approach relocated a classical play to some later time and place, thereby demonstrating its "relevance" through a more contemporary environment. Updating was the style usually associated with Michael Benthall's Old Vic and the Stratford Shakespeare Theatre in Connecticut and the early Guthrie Theatre in Minneapolis. Guthrie himself called this process "jollying Shakespeare up."

Jollying Shakespeare up gave us such novelties as a *Measure for Measure* set in Freud's Vienna, a *Much Ado About Nothing* relocated to Spanish Texas, and a *Troilus and Cressida* occurring during the American Civil War—creating geographical transplants that managed to provide visual surprise and an illusion of immediacy without any particular insight into the heart of the play. (To my shame, I myself once directed a production of *Macbeth* set in Stonehenge, featuring extra-terrestrial witches.) Updating was an improvement on traditional Shakespeare, but it was nevertheless a visual and histrionic act rather than a metaphorical and imaginative one. I preferred an approach that would navigate between the Scylla of dry academicism and the Charybdis of empty fashion.

A few of my colleagues thought I had taken leave of my senses, among them John Simon, who believed that classical plays should be produced on stage exactly as they were originally written. My old friend Harold Bloom, battered by bad productions, preferred the theatre in his head, often wondering aloud whether his beloved Shakespeare should be on stage at all. I sympathized with Bloom's frustration, but obviously plays have no real life unless embodied in the flesh of living actors. And to satisfy Simon's demand for "original intentions," Shakespeare's women would have to be played by boys and his Cleopatra would be required to wear a hoop skirt. To me, these were prescriptions for embalming the classics in formaldehyde.

Partly as a result of such debates, we were beginning to witness major changes in classical production. While traditional and updated approaches continued to hold the stage, the succeeding years also saw the rise of the *auteur* director, claiming the same freedom in regard to theatre texts as the movie director had with screenplays. The result was a host of brilliantly reconstituted and recalibrated, if highly controversial, productions. Among the most celebrated of these (after Brook's original forays) were Andrei Gregory's *Endgame* set in a cage to emphasize its claustral atmosphere, performed in a vaudeville style punctuated by old movie comedy soundtracks (some years later at the American Repertory Theatre JoAnne Akalaitis would scandalize the playwright by placing *Endgame* in an abandoned subway station in order to literalize its post-nuclear subtext); Andrei Şerban's *Fragments of a Trilogy* at La Mama, composed of three Greek tragedies returned to their choreographed ritual roots, not to mention a host of other brilliant Şerban reinterpretations, including his postindustrial *Cherry Orchard* for Papp's Lincoln Center and his *commedia dell'arte King Stag* for the ART; and preeminently Ingmar Bergman's totalitarian *Hamlet* and brutalized *Peer Gynt*, indeed any classical play he chose to put his inspired hand to.

The reinterpretation of classical plays became such a popular activity in ensuing decades that it began to attract directors not normally interested in such material; Lee Breuer of Mabou Mines staged a controversial version of *The Tempest* at the New York Shakespeare Festival (codirected by Ruth Maleczech) that had actors imitating Mae West, W. C. Fields, and Sid Vicious. Robert Woodruff, Sam Shepard's chief director, contributed the first of his numerous classical reinterpretations, a Lincoln Center *Comedy of Errors* featuring the Flying Karamazovs doing a juggling act. Alvin Epstein, previously known best as an actor, contributed a production of *A Midsummer Night's Dream* at Yale and the ART based on the Purcell/Dryden opera and the combat paintings of Uccello; Ron Daniels gave us a *Hamlet* where the title character played by Mark Rylance spent the whole play in his pajamas, while an army of new young American directors, including Karin Coonrod, James Lapine, Anne Bogart, Emily Mann, Brian Kulick, Liz Diamond, Bill Rauch, Darko Tresnjak, and many others began embracing classical plays as a way of exercising new creative muscles. I even managed to persuade the celebrated auteur Robert Wilson to do his first classical productions—Euripides' *Alcestis* and Ibsen's *When We*

Dead Awaken—after which he became as devoted to classical plays and operas as to his own original creations.

Such productions were enough to persuade me that reinterpreted classics were the highway to a new theatrical Eden. But it was not long before the garden was being blighted by a trace of plant mold. In 1968 the Living Theatre returned to these shores, after a nomadic period in Europe, bringing *Paradise Now, The Mysteries,* and *Frankenstein.* But despite the fact that its repertory featured one classic play, *Antigone,* reinterpreted as an indictment of the Johnson administration and the Vietnam War, the company that, before its exile, had staged Brecht, Lorca, Cocteau, and Pirandello now appeared to have lost its stomach for written plays and playwrights. During a New York symposium in the early seventies, Judith Malina announced that she would much rather play Judith Malina than Hedda Gabler, and she was soon seconded by one of her actors shouting his own scholarly opinion of the classics—"Fuck Shakespeare. Fuck Euripides." During the same period, Richard Schechner and The Performance Group transformed *The Bacchae* into a group grope called *Dionysus in 69* (curiously reminiscent of The Living's writhing *Paradise Now*), and it was growing obvious that classical theatre was being used less as an opportunity for understanding human destiny than as an invitation for physical intimacy between actors and spectators, in the chummy fashion of the time.

I look back on this age as a period of theatrical self-absorption, one that left a permanent imprint on our stage. Radical theatre had turned into a mode of institutionalized narcissism where the self-indulgent fantasies of directors and actors were often being substituted for the intentions of the play. Previous experimentalists had also taken great liberties with texts, but when the great Russian Meyerhold did a surrealist version of, say, Gogol's *The Inspector General*, he was primarily trying to expose its dreamlike roots. Now the production apparatus was replacing, rather than reinforcing, the playwright's function, and the text was becoming a springboard for subjective directorial journeys. "To the tumbrels with the author," as the critic Kenneth Tynan described it, after threatening to apply a lighted match to the bare feet of the next naked actor who clambered over his lap.

Under the influence of The Living Theatre and The Performance Group, and to some extent Grotowski's Poor Theatre, with its actor-generated classics like *The Constant Prince*, the emphasis had begun to fall on the gesture rather than the word, on physical rather than vocal projection. Even Peter Brook was abandoning the process he had done so much to advance. Having produced a Living Theatre-type protest exercise with the Royal Shakespeare Company called *US* in 1966, Brook departed England to set up his own experimental group in Paris, called the International Centre of Theatre Research. There he began working on a series of projects that were more likely to be adaptations of nontheatrical works than written plays, though poets like Ted Hughes sometimes contributed dialogue. The results were group-created projects, usually adapted from religious or sociological or anthropological or psychological tracts, like *The Mahabharata*, *The Conference of the Birds*, *The Ik*, and *The Man Who Mistook His Wife for a Hat*. Only occasionally would a Brook season include a classic play such as *The Cherry Orchard* (played on a Persian carpet) or *Hamlet* (drastically cut).

Brook's influence, along with the lingering influence of performance groups, has been incalculable on modern theatre. But in my opinion, and I should emphasize that mine was a minority opinion, his international company, expertly trained though it was, seemed to me less devoted to artistic communication than to group therapy, less concerned with dramatic breakthroughs than with inspirational statements about world brotherhood. To my mind, Brook had replaced the director's chair with the guru's rug. And I thought I detected a touch of neocolonialism in the way he was arranging so many different nationalities, cultures, and languages on the same stage. I longed for the director who had once reimagined great plays, who had managed to evolve a magnificent *Marat/Sade* out of workshops on the Theatre of Cruelty (Artaud and Genet), and who had taught us how the works of the past could be seen afresh through the lens of contemporary playwriting.

In short, four decades after my original article, I am ready to concede that the postmodern movement may have gone too far and that, instead of helping to illuminate classical plays, the auteur director is often obfuscating and obscuring them.

And this puts us in danger of losing our connection to classical theatre. Do I sound like a cranky old conservative, abandoning my previous commitment to radical reinterpretations and joining a chorus of critical naysayers? Perhaps. But I am hardly calling for the abolition of auteurism. I am simply suggesting alternative approaches that maintain the integrity of a classic, neither by freezing nor misreading it, but by reviving its original energies. The great plays of the past still have much to teach us—about the fallibility of leaders and the fickleness of followers, about the nobility and brutality of human nature, about the sometimes tortured relations between the sexes, about the impact of destiny on the individual will, and, indeed, about every possible kind of human transaction. Most classical productions today are showing no interest in those issues or are failing to clarify them. More masterpieces, please.

(2008)

Weill, Lenya, and the Broadway Musical

Love Song: The Lives of Kurt Weill and Lotte Lenya is the title Ethan Mordden gives to his new book on two major twentieth-century musical artists, but it is somewhat misleading.

The relationship between Weill and Lenya was less a pulsating romance than a very practical partnership, not so much a passionate love song as one of Weill's melancholy Mandalay ballads. This is not to suggest that the couple's feelings for each other were lacking in tenderness. Their marriage was nourished by deep personal emotions and mutual tastes. But Lenya, who enjoyed a brief career as a teenage prostitute, was compulsively unfaithful to Weill throughout their lives together, both with men and with women. She also left Weill once for a tenor, later remarried him, and then, after his death, married two more men, both of them gay.

Lenya's German biographer, Jens Rosteck, considers most of Lenya's erotic adventures to have been rehearsals for her performance career. Talk about actor preparation! Whatever the case, they hardly display the amorous longings of a Juliet or an Isolde. A more accurate way to describe the Weill-Lenya relationship, from Mordden's account of it, is as a friendly affiliation between two Germanic professionals (Lenya an Austrian, Weill a Jew), between a serious composer and a cabaret artist, whose careers were mutually supportive and who shared the same language, values, tastes, politics, friendships, and musical projects, if not always the same bed.

Of the two, Kurt Weill may have been the more gifted, but Lenya was unquestionably the more dynamic. Indeed, their relationship struck me as reflecting the kind of symbiosis one often finds between composers and lyricists, in which the style and content of a song is usually determined by the wordsmith (or singer in Lenya's case), even though it is the songwriter who usually provides its emotional imprint.

A classic example of this lopsided partnership is the way the musical personality of Richard Rodgers transformed after the death of his first Broadway collaborator. As the creative partner of the gay sophisticate Lorenz Hart, Rodgers wrote music vibrating with urban electricity—highly witty, often cynical, sometimes erotic—whereas, collaborating with the exurbanite Bucks County landlord, Oscar Hammerstein II, his music became considerably more sunny, wholesome, chaste, and rustic. Rodgers wrote "The Lady is a Tramp" with Hart, "My Girl Back Home" with Hammerstein, "Bewitched, Bothered, and Bewildered" with Hart, "How Do You Solve a Problem Like Maria" with Hammerstein, "Ship Without a Sail" with Hart, "Surrey with the Fringe on Top" with Hammerstein, "Manhattan," with Hart, and "Oklahoma" with Hammerstein.

There are, of course, a number of songwriters who managed to sustain their own style, whatever the contribution of the lyricist; Cole Porter, Frank Loesser, and Stephen Sondheim are the most obvious examples. But these are composers who normally served as their own lyricists or—in the case of Loesser—lyricists who later wrote their own music. More often, Broadway musicals were created by chameleons like Jerome Kern who could accommodate virtually any lyric writer—P. G. Wodehouse ("Bill"), Oscar Hammerstein II ("Can't Help Lovin' Dat Man"), Dorothy Fields ("The Way You Look Tonight"), Johnny Mercer ("I'm Old-Fashioned"), and Ira Gershwin ("Long Ago and Far Away")—with songs so varied you were at a loss to identify a single artistic source.

As for Irving Berlin, who also wrote his own lyrics, he didn't change his style so much as he did his own character, adopting a new idiom, temperament, and set of holidays as a result of his expatriation. Over the 90 years that he wrote songs—He died at 101.—this Russian-born Jew morphed into an American patriot ("God Bless America," "This is the Army, Mr. Jones"), a Wild West hillbilly ("Annie Get Your Gun"), and a celebrant of Christian holy days ("I'm Dreaming of a White Christmas," "Easter Parade"). I mention this to dramatize the flexible nature of composers. Even Mozart changed course after the sequence of ironic, lighthearted operas that he wrote with Leonardo Da Ponte—*La Nozze di Figaro*, *Cosí fan Tutte*, and *Don Giovanni*—when he collaborated on the more stately *Die Zauberflöte* with Emanuel Schikaneder.

Like all such generalizations, this one is open to many exceptions—the most obvious ones being George Gershwin, who only worked with his brother Ira, and the irrepressible Leonard Bernstein whose brassy style remained the same, regardless of his lyricists. I propose it as a path into the debate over why Kurt Weill changed course so radically after he and Lenya left Europe, a step ahead of the Nazis, to transplant themselves in American soil. As Mordden, a competent if splashy student of German culture tells us, Weil's major European influences were essentially the avant-garde classical composers Schoenberg and Busoni—under whose atonal shadows he wrote his two symphonies—and the left-wing dramatists, Georg Kaiser and Bertolt Brecht, who influenced his theatre style.

It was Brecht, of course, with whom we are most likely to associate Weill. He certainly had the greatest influence on Weill's career. The Brecht-Weill collaboration produced some of the most dazzling musical theatre works of the twentieth century, among them *Aufstieg und Fall der Stadt Mahagonny* (*The Rise and Fall of the City of Mahagonny*), *Die Dreigroschenoper* (*The Threepenny Opera*), *The Seven Deadly Sins*, and—though Brecht played only a nominal part in writing it—*Happy End*. Working with Brecht was undoubtedly the most significant event in Weill's career; their union is almost as well-known today as the musical marriage of Gilbert and Sullivan.

Mordden, like the Brecht biographer John Fuegi, does not have a very high regard for the German dramatist. He is almost obsessive in the vituperative ways he harps on Brecht's vituperative ways ("The same ranting and shrieking associated with Hitler."), his body odor ("Brecht bathed so seldom and smoked cheap cigars so incessantly that he was all

but unbearable in the physical sense."), his left-wing politics
("a foul piece of grown-up propaganda"), and his egotism
(or "drama-queen personality"). He concludes: "Brecht never
stopped stealing, never stopped screaming, and never stopped
stooging for the totalitarian crushing of the human spirit, as
long as the crushing was performed by communists instead
of Nazis." He is equally dismissive of Brecht's wife, Helene
Weigel, whom he calls "the least attractive of Brecht's Eves
in every sense, a talented performer but an angry loon whose
only content was Communist fanaticism." He doesn't mention that Wiegel eventually became one of the great German
actresses of the century, the creator of Mother Courage's
trademark "silent scream."

It is true that Weigel served as a "kitchen slave" to Brecht
in his Hollywood years, while her husband continued to accu-
mulate mistresses, whom Mordden (like Fuegi) believes wrote
a lot of his plays. He also believes it was the "fanatical" Weigel
who converted the "progressive" Brecht to Communism.
(She certainly contributed to the failure of Happy End by
reading Communist propaganda aloud at the curtain call!)
But if we had to measure works of art by the characters of
their authors, libraries would lock up their stacks. Brecht
did have most of the defects attributed to him, including a
notable disinclination to criticize Stalinism. But, with a few
exceptions, his work is usually too complicated to be reduced
to political dogma, and his plays rarely display the kind of
political reductionism associated with ideologues. (More
typical are his ambiguous endings like the powerless "Help"
that concludes The Good Woman of Setzuan or the finale of
Mother Courage when the title character, having lost all her
children to a forty-year war, drags her cart around the stage in
ever-widening circles.) For a more detached view of Brecht's
achievement, readers would be advised to turn to scholars
such as Eric Bentley (whom Mordden mentions only once)

and Martin Esslin (whom he doesn't mention at all). It was Bentley who accurately compared Brecht to the poet Dubedat in Shaw's *Candida*: "A scoundrel but an artist."

Mordden is occasionally willing to concede value to the Brecht-Weill canon, sometimes even to Brecht's genius ("a unique contributor to the body of theatre work in Western Civilization"). But he is much more concerned with the defects in Brecht's character, even charging him with being a "destroyer of productions," though it was Brecht who founded and directed the Berliner Ensemble from 1949 to 1956. If Brecht contributed no new plays to his theatre, he led an acting company almost unparalleled in the world, even if largely devoted to showcasing his own past work.

For all Mordden's lip service to Brecht's talent, he seems impatient for Weill to divorce this Weimar liability and remarry the healthier muse of American musical comedy. Despite his apparent familiarity with German culture, Mordden has done most of his previously published work on Broadway musicals, including a six-volume history of the form, from the 1920s through the 1970s, plus a book about Florenz Ziegfeld. You don't need a tuning fork to know the pitch of this author's musical preferences, and although he can grudgingly praise some of Weill's Weimar achievements, he seems more eager to defend him against charges of Broadway commercialism. Explaining, for example, why Lee Strasberg, who directed the Paul Green-Kurt Weill *Johnny Johnson* for the Group Theatre, considered it "a play without music," he writes: "It was mandatory at the time for anyone with intellectual pretensions to scorn musicals as meretricious."

I'm not prepared to defend Lee Strasberg, who was probably tone deaf, but as an unappointed spokesman for this intellectually pretentious club (formerly known as highbrows), let me say that we don't consider musicals "meretricious."

We consider most of them underachieved and overpraised. Many intellectuals celebrate the union between high art and low art as personified, for example, by Shakespeare, Moliere, Charlie Chaplin, Samuel Beckett, and Brecht and Weill. What doesn't make us so happy is Broadway pandering and middlebrow pretense.

Mordden typifies the overinflation of the Broadway musical's reputation, comparing, for example, "the revolutionary flowering of the musical" to "the overthrowing of the Russian autocracy." What next? The Storming of the Bastille? The Battle of Waterloo? The entertainment value of the form, and, in more rare cases, its artistic value—the Lerner-Loewe *My Fair Lady*, for example, or the Boublil-Schönberg *Les Mes*, or Sondheim's *Passion*—is not to be underestimated. But the bulk of Broadway musicals, a form chauvinistically designated not just as revolutionary but as "America's native art form," would be more accurately categorized as a species of entertainment, similar to the tradition of Viennese operetta from which it descended.

Kurt Weill's book writers and lyricists when he finally emigrated to this country in the early thirties included a lot of gifted people, such as Franz Werfel (*The Eternal Road*, 1934), Paul Green (*Johnny Johnson*, 1936), Elmer Rice and Langston Hughes (*Street Scene*), Moss Hart and Ira Gershwin (*Lady in the Dark*, 1941; *The Firebrand of Florence*, 1945), S. J. Perelman and Ogden Nash (*One Touch of Venus*, 1943), Alan Jay Lerner (*Love Life*, 1948), and, most compatibly, Maxwell Anderson (*Knickerbocker Holiday*, 1938 and *Lost in the Stars*, 1949).

It was with Anderson that Weill wrote some of his most wistful Broadway music, most notably "The September Song" from *Knickerbocker Holiday* and the title song of *Lost in the Stars*. But virtually all of Weill's American music is invested with sweet nostalgia that you will not often find in his early orchestral compositions or in his work with Brecht. Just compare the ruthlessness of "Pirate Jenny" from *Der Dreigro-schenoper* ("Then they'll pile up the bodies/And I'll say,/ That'll learn ya") with the bounciness of "Saga of Jenny" from *Lady in the Dark* ("Jenny made her mind up when she was three. She herself was going to trim the Christmas tree"). These two Jennys belong in completely different universes.

Early in his book, Mordden writes, "A common inter-pretation of Weill reads him as a shape-shifter, working in prestigiously 'difficult' political art in Germany and then, in America, going commercial, as if the political were inherently prestigious." Incensed by what he later calls "the relentless hectoring by critics at the way Weill supposedly changes his style from uniquely German to stereotypically American," he adds that this "ignores the central fact that he changes his style from work to work." Mordden goes on: "Yes, Weill was a shape-shifter, but throughout his career, not just when he crossed the Atlantic." I think it is possible to agree with Mordden's high estimate of Weill's Broadway work and still recognize that the work he did with the immoral, malodorous, Communist stooge Brecht was deeper, darker, and denser than anything he ever produced with his freshly scrubbed Broadway colleagues.

Indeed, Weill's meeting with Brecht produced what many, including myself, consider the high moment of twentieth-century musical theatre. (Mordden identifies it as the moment "Weill suddenly starts acting sexy!") Their work together culminated in one of the greatest modern operas in the canon, namely *Aufstieg und Fall der Stadt Mahagonny* (*The Rise and Fall of the City of Mahagonny*, 1930). Even the Broadway-besotted Mordden concedes that *Mahagonny* is "Weill's finest work," though he is not altogether trustworthy about the opera's American production history.[1]

Weill's work on *Mahagonny* contains the same stylistic turns you find in all his Brecht collaborations: the minor key atonality, the tinny syncopations, the spasmodic rhythms, the dreamlike jazz of America, and the melancholy climax when Jimmy Mahoney's life ends on the gallows. (Even Brecht's supposedly happy endings are bitter, as, for example, the finale of *The Seven Deadly Sins*, when the two Annas finally complete their "kleines Haus am Mississippi in Louisiana" by rejecting anything that might bring them emotional satisfaction.)

Brecht believed that human beings were driven by greed, which was rational, and by sexual desire, which was sensual, and this made your capacity to rise in the world subject to your capacity to suppress decent feelings. That is why his characters—the two sides of the Good Person of Szechwan, Shen Te and Shui Ta, for example, not to mention the two Annas in *Seven Deadly Sins*—are often split.

It is doubtful whether Weill shared Brecht's double nature, though Lenya certainly pulled him apart from time to time. Mordden pays far less attention to Lenya's professional life than he does to her husband's, but his admiration for her is, nonetheless, almost starstruck, possibly because he finds her so compatible with his aesthetic. He calls Lenya "the Empress of Brechtian mischief" and "a musical comedy Mother Courage" and reserves his greatest praise for the parts she played in Hollywood movies and Broadway shows. But her "Surabaya Johnny" from *Happy End* and her "Benares Song" from *Mahagonny-Songspiel* probe far deeper than the admittedly delicious turn she did as a lesbian double agent in *From Russia with Love*, chasing 007 around the room, kicking at him with a poisoned knife blade hidden in her shoe. And her performance as the singing Anna I in the City Center Ballet version of *The Seven Deadly Sins* left a more powerful impression on many of us than her admittedly fine characterization of Fraulein Schneider in the Kander and Ebb *I Am a Camera* recreation of Weimer culture in *Cabaret*, possibly because it was original rather than an imitation.

Speaking of split natures, let me say a few words about the author's literary style. It is as if two different people were writing his book. There are times when Mordden's voice sounds like something overheard at Sardi's: "There was nothing in the European world like being the author of a smash-hit opera." Sometimes it sounds like a press agent's release: "That is the Kurt Weill we know, leading his band of musical cutthroats in spoof operas that laugh about sex and tear down your heroes, Public Composer Number One on the Nazis' enemies list." When Weill falls in love with Lenya, Mordden writes, "He does everything but break into 'Younger than Springtime.'" "*Mother Courage*," he says as if in praise, "unfolds as inexorably as anything by Sardou." (Apparently he is unaware that Sardou is generally considered a mechanical Boulevard artist.)

And yet, despite the number of editorial errors and stylistic blunders scattered throughout the book, there are times when the writing becomes almost elegant, as if a teacher of English Composition had pushed his way into Mordden's study and brandished a cane at him. His description of Weimar Berlin, for example, the world of Georg Grosz and Fritz Lang and Marlene Dietrich, is hauntingly evoked. And he can be funny about the milieu of German show business: "The Diva walkout, along with The Other Diva's Refusal to Sing a Solo Because It Is Beneath Her, the Mechanical Failure of a Special Effect, the Risible Vanity of the Leading Man, and the Kibitzers at the Dress Rehearsal Who Gleefully Predict the Greatest Flop in History were all part of the milieu that Weill was entering for the first time." But he can also be unfeelingly tasteless: "Ira had been so crushed by the untimely death of his brother George that he had folded into retirement in Los Angeles as the Widow Gershwin."

The mixture of clarity and vulgarity that permeates Mordden's book on Weill and Lenya is suggestive of the underlying nature of middlebrow taste. But even to use such terms as highbrow, middlebrow, and lowbrow these days is to suggest that one is stuck in some prehistoric era. I think I can pinpoint the period when these distinctions began to blur, because I recently came across a 1957 theatre review by Diana Trilling in which she compared O'Neill's *Long Day's Journey Into Night* (in the memorable Quintero production) with the Lerner-Loewe musical *My Fair Lady* and preferred the latter. "I have never admired the plays of Eugene O'Neill," she wrote, "and I confess what is no doubt a morbid resistance to works of the imagination which deal with unpleasant themes." Now her husband Lionel's continuing distaste for O'Neill (not to mention theatre in general) was based on the playwright's clunky, inarticulate early drama, not the later masterpieces. Would he or Diana have applied the same measuring stick to novels with "unpleasant themes" such as *Madame Bovary, The Possessed,* or *As I Lay Dying?* When Diana reluctantly decided to last out the performance, she found the experience rather rewarding, though she wished the show had been a great deal shorter.

Diana Trilling writes that "perhaps the best compliment I can pay O'Neill is to acknowledge that his autobiographical drama had for me an import almost as large and lasting as a superb musical comedy." Regardless of the genuine artistry of *My Fair Lady,* to read a sentence like this, which patronizes what is perhaps the greatest American play in the canon, is to see a brilliant intellectual masquerading as a Philistine housewife. In this, she resembles a lot of educated people these days, perfectly capable of appreciating great literature, who only visit the stage to see a Broadway musical with a Hollywood star. And that is one reason why so much of our sorry theatre seems so depressing and disappointing and why so much of the writing about it does, too.

(2013)

Thornton Wilder:
The Paleface Who Wanted to Be a Redskin

Thornton Niven Wilder, author of seven novels and nine plays, was born in 1897 in Madison, Wisconsin, the grandson of a Presbyterian clergyman and the son of a government diplomat who later became a newspaper editor. Best known for *Our Town*, a homespun story of domestic life in a small New England village, he has always been considered a quintessential middle-American writer.

But as Penelope Niven's painstaking new biography, *Thornton Wilder: A Life*, helps make clear, Wilder, though fiercely loyal to his country, his family, and his wide circle of American friends, was a man with powerful literary ambitions who felt more affinity with European classics and the contemporary avant-garde than with anything in the native canon. Among his primary literary and philosophical influences were not Emerson, Longfellow, or Frost, as one might expect of such an intrinsically New England figure, but Kierkegaard, Nietzsche, Kafka, Proust, and Joyce, and he was also deeply indebted to the drama of the Greeks and the Spanish Golden Age. (Wilder once devoted years of precious writing time, ten hours a day, to dating the five hundred plays of Lope de Vega.)

He was a small-town boy who travelled widely in the world after spending his early years in China. In his trips abroad he became friendly with some of the leading international figures of the period, including Hemingway, Fitzgerald, Freud, Mann, Picasso, Ezra Pound, Edmund Wilson, and Gertrude Stein. (Indeed, he might have been a template for the celebrity-dazzled hero of Woody Allen's *Midnight in Paris*.) At the same time, he was cultivating friendships with a host of American luminaries from Alexander Wolcott to Henry Luce, from Robert Hutchins, President of the University of Chicago, to the heavyweight champion of the world,

Gene Tunney. (He also became friendly with the eighteen-year-old Orson Welles, who often claimed that Wilder had discovered him.)

These relationships and influences are reflected in the relatively radical forms of his books and plays. He experimented for a while with Dada and fell under the spell of Existentialism. *The Skin of our Teeth* is so heavily indebted to *Finnegans Wake* that the Joyce scholars, Joseph Campbell and Henry Morton Robinson—authors of *A Skeleton Guide to Finnegans Wake*—once charged him, in a two-part article in the *Saturday Review of Literature*, with plagiarism. *Our Town*, with its bare stage and direct address, its expository Stage Manager, and its experimentation with theatrical space and time, owes a significant debt to Pirandello's *Six Characters in Search of an Author*. *The Merchant of Yonkers*—an adaptation that mutated first into *The Matchmaker* and later into the spectacularly successful musical *Hello Dolly*—is based on a nineteenth-century Austrian farce by Johann Nestroy with additional scenes from Molière. Wilder's novel, *The Bridge on the Luis Rey*, was inspired by the nineteenth-century French playwright and short story writer, Prosper Mérimée. His play, *The Alcestiad*, and his novel, *The Woman of Andros*, both owe their existence to Greek and Roman models, namely Euripides, Menander, and Terence.

Wilder was also attracted to experimental European auteurs like Max Reinhardt and Richard Boleslawsky, each of whom took a turn at botching one of his plays when the obvious directors for such fundamentally native material were locals like Jed Harris, who staged *Our Town*, and Elia Kazan who directed *The Skin of Our Teeth*. (The latter had a stunning cast, headed by Frederic March, Florence Eldridge, and the husky-voiced Tallulah Bankhead as Sabina the maid.)

To me, the most puzzling thing about Thornton Wilder has always been the disparity between his radical European and classical forms and his rather bland domestic themes. Niven, who writes like an admiring family member (and possibly is one—Niven is Wilder's middle name as well as the maiden name of his mother), has composed a biography that greatly increases my respect for the humanity and decency of this good man, if not for most of his work. Like two of his four siblings, he never married, but he was an obedient son and solicitous brother, a devoted friend, and generous to all who approached him. He contributed large amounts of money toward the hospitalizations of his father, right up until his death, and to his sister, Charlotte, after she suffered an extended mental breakdown. He was always ready with advice and even financial help for students and strangers. And despite an accumulation of accolades and prizes that would have turned the head of Zeno of Citium (the founder of Stoicism), his modesty was legendary. The writer with whom he might be best compared regarding the reticence and sympathy of his nature is Anton Chekhov.

Cosmopolitan in his influences, he was nevertheless a native child in his optimistic belief that humanity was basically decent and redeemable and that fictional characters should embody these qualities. Wilder's decorum toward his creations led the militant Communist watchdog Michael Gold to attack him in *The New Republic* as "the Emily Post of culture," dismissing the figures in his first novel, *The Cabala*, as "some eccentric old aristocrats in Rome, seen through the eyes of a typical American art 'pansy.'" Wilder was deeply hurt by Gold's comments but, as was his habit, refused to retaliate.

He served in two world wars, one of which included a Holocaust, and yet the sounds that usually reverberated in this veteran's ears were not cries of suffering but anthems of affirmation, not unlike Anne Frank's stubborn belief "in spite of everything, that people are truly good at heart." He was not above occasional reflections on the more carnal side of human nature. (He once affirmed that the hidden metaphor of *Finnegans Wake* was buggery.) But only toward the end of his life did he begin to yield up some of his conviction that the world was grounded in love. His penultimate novel, *The Eighth Day*, which some believe to be his masterpiece, hopefully prophesies a fundamental change in human character: "We are at the beginning of the second week. We are the children of the eighth day." That new day was meant to signal a transformation similar to that of Darwin's species into Nietzsche's Übermenschen. But even Wilder seemed astonished at the disparity between his ambition and his achievement. As he remarked about the novel, "It's as though *Little Women* were being mulled over by Dostoyevsky."

The critic Philip Rahv once drew a useful distinction between literary figures he called "palefaces" and those he identified as "redskins." His purpose was to distinguish work like "the drawing-room fictions of Henry James" from "the open-air poems of Walt Whitman," between writers with a cultivated literary style and those driven by a fiery radical temperament. Surely, Wilder's work is of the former, more genial kind. It is not a barbaric yawp that resounds in his pages so much as a homespun drawl. Even if you compare *Our Town*, for example, with works from a similar American genre, like Sinclair Lewis's *Main Street* or Edgar Lee Masters's *Spoon River Anthology*, Wilder displays none of the edge of these writers who are usually too jaundiced about small-town life ever to become fixtures in the high-school reading list. (*Our Town*, by contrast, has now received more student productions than almost any other play in history and is regularly revived on Broadway about once every five years.) Wilder often used cosmological ideas to describe domestic behavior: "the life of a village against the life of the stars." But there is a real question whether this author, in works like *Our Town*, actually succeeded in his ambition "to raise ordinary daily conversation between ordinary people to the level of universal human experience," or whether he simply invented another homiletic genre.

The unkindest comment on this discrepancy, of course, continues to be Kenneth Tynan's wicked treatment of the play as if it were written in the context of William Faulkner's *The Hamlet*: "Well, folks," drawls Tynan's parody of Wilder's Stage Manager,

> Reckon that's about it. End of another day in the city of Jefferson, Yoknapatawpha County, Mississippi. Nothin' much happened. Couple of people got raped, couple more got their teeth kicked in, but way up there those far away old stars are still doing their old cosmic crisscross, and there ain't a thing we can do about it . . . Down behind the morgue a few of the young people are roastin' a nigger over an open fire, but I guess every town has its night owls, and afore long they'll be tucked up asleep like anybody else. Nothin' stirring down at the big old plantation house—you can't even hear the hummin' of the electrified barbed-wire fence, 'cause last night some drunk ran slap into it and fused the whole works.

The satiric contrast, of course, is between the vanilla-soda virtues of George and Emily in Grover's Corners and the virulent, racist fever of the Snopes family in Jefferson, Mississippi. Wilder's New England village seems utopian precisely because it is immune from any of the evils afflicting America at that time. "Oh earth," says Emily at the end of the play, sounding like a small-town Candide, "you're too wonderful for anybody to realize you." In this best of all possible villages there is no persecution, no lynching, no religious prejudice, no union busting, no gross income inequality, no sign of the Know-Nothings who would later become the Tea Party—just wholesome meals of roast turkey, homogenized milk, and Wonder Bread loaves being served by kindly beaming folk out of Norman Rockwell portraits. (Wilder actually collected his one-act plays under a title that might have been appropriate for a Rockwell painting—*The Long Christmas Dinner*.)

Tynan's parody is especially cruel when you consider how often Wilder himself played the Stage Manager in productions of his play. (The cover of his biography features a photo of the author in the part, sitting on a stool, looking like a kindly general practitioner about to palpate your chest.) But Tynan's implication that the author of *Our Town* was indifferent to human suffering is simply not true. Wilder's compassion was infinite, and there was not a prejudiced bone in his body. He only seems to have had one serious quarrel in his entire life—with a director over the liberties he took with his text—and even that was resolved amicably. But his decision to write about an American town so homogenous in its population, so lacking in serious urban problems, has made the play a prime target for satire, though the scene in which Emily returns from the grave to savor a day on earth is unquestionably very moving. Persistently liberal in his voting habits, Thornton seems to have been insulated from social outrage. Savage indignation did not lacerate his breast.

Tolstoy has famously observed (in *Anna Karenina*) that "happy families are all alike; every unhappy family is unhappy in its own way." It was Wilder's limitation as an artist that he preferred to write mostly about happy families. Imagine Eugene O'Neill or Edward Albee calling a play *The Happy Journey from Trenton to Camden*. Indeed, imagine Kafka or Joyce writing a line like this from Wilder's novel, *Heaven is My Destination*: "You know what I think is the greatest thing in the world? It's when a man, I mean an American, sits down at dinner with his wife and six children around him."

Years ago, Steven Marcus summed up the dominant theme of Charles Dickens in one telling phrase: "Family life—a nightmare." But in the works of Wilder, family life is almost always a postprandial daydream. "I have decided," he once proclaimed somewhat loftily, "that the human race can be given the benefit of the doubt." Catastrophe is hardly a missing element in his work. The Antrobus family in *The Skin of our Teeth*, for example, goes through the Ice Age, The Flood, and the Apocalypse, among other disasters. But they almost never lose their irrepressible good cheer and bubbly good nature. (Indeed, I suspect the amiable twenty-thousand-year-old Mr. Antrobus may have been a model for Mel Brooks's huggable but more obviously counterfeit 2,000 Year Old Man.)

To navigate the deep chasm between the nature of the writer and the disposition of his writings, Penelope Niven's compendious account of Wilder's complicated personality is an indispensable guide. The author spent ten years examining a massive collection of Wilder's diaries, journals, and almost daily correspondence, leaving virtually no incident of his life unrecorded, however trivial. The result is a work that makes previous biographies by Richard H. Goldstone, Gilbert Harrison, and Linda Simon look skimpy by comparison. In combination with the three-volume Library of America edition of Wilder's collected plays, novels, and writings on the theatre (edited by J. D. McClatchy), Niven's exhaustive research represents a complete guide for any Wilder explorer, if—at over eight hundred pages—perhaps a little more exhausting than exhaustive for the general reader. What emerges from this book is the story of a man whose life was full of incident, but oddly empty of drama, whose childhood, surprisingly, seemed less like a long Christmas dinner than like an extended Lenten fast.

In short, Wilder's family life was not happy, and the many beaming parents and children in his plays seem to have been a form of wish fulfillment. The major source of early tension for Wilder was his father, a Puritan disciplinarian with a missionary's zeal who was continually hectoring his five children to lead upright, conventional lives. "I am praying that the decadence in high-minded youth I know so well may not be yours," he writes in a manner that Niven correctly compares to Polonius lecturing Laertes, "Faithfully economize at every point, and have money to pay your bills in full. . . . Then you will earn the respect of your father."

Wilder, who was later more inclined to respect and love his bottle, was nevertheless forced by this autocratic parent to take the pledge at age fifteen. His father also influenced his choice of schools and colleges—first Oberlin, then Yale—as well as his course of study. And considering that Thornton loved the theatre above all the arts, he could hardly have been encouraged by his father's Puritan belief—according to Thornton's sister Isabel—that the theatre is "an agent of evil and degeneration." Yet, the New Haven area, where his father became an editor at the *Journal-Courier*, remained Wilder's American base for most of his life. He taught and served as housemaster at prep schools like Lawrenceville but then lectured and gave commencement addresses at Yale—when he wasn't traveling throughout Europe in search of advanced culture, highbrow intellectuals, and avant-garde artists.

The effect of his father's influence, not to mention his mother's reclusiveness, on his four siblings was even more powerful. His brother, Amos, became a preacher and later a professor at the Yale Divinity School after suffering a nervous breakdown in 1934. Despite such setbacks, Amos and his youngest sister, Janet, at least raised families. His two other sisters, like Thornton, remained unmarried throughout their lifetimes, Isabel choosing to remain near her parents in New Haven. (She also chose that city to be near Thornton, whom she worshipped throughout her life and tried to emulate as a novelist.) His oldest sister, Charlotte, a poet with uncon-summated lesbian tendencies, had a serious schizophrenic meltdown and spent years in mental institutions undergoing therapy, shock treatments, and, finally, a lobotomy, like the sister of Tennessee Williams.

As for Thornton, his sex life was hardly vigorous. It is something on which Niven, who occasionally resembles a Victorian biographer, seems hesitant to dwell. ("He left very little evidence of that very private matter.") Wilder had occasional flirtations with female admirers, often older women. He appeared to enjoy some physical intimacy with the actor Glenn Hunter in 1918. Somebody broke his heart in 1925 but was never identified. And in 1993, a columnist named Samuel Stewart confessed to an extended affair with the author, adding that Wilder was "afraid of sex and unfortunately I was put in the position of outing him but I never did until after he had died." Other gay men, who were friendly with Wilder at the time, all agreed that, whatever his sexual disposition, "his personal life was intensely private, seemingly impervious to rumor."

This is not to say that Wilder didn't enjoy a number of warm personal relationships. "The only two things in the world that are rewarding," he once wrote to Gertrude Stein, "are the masterpieces of the fine arts and one's friends." (He pointedly says nothing about family.) But Niven is probably correct to conclude that, while Wilder's friendships were legion, sex didn't play a very crucial role in them. Compared, say, with Tennessee Williams, whose homosexuality may have been disguised in his plays but hardly absent from his life, he might have been a Franciscan monk—I mean a celibate one—and his chaste conduct colored his treatment of romantic relationships in his fiction. In Williams, castration, rape, mutilation, and murder are virtually instruments of the plots. Wilder substitutes the sizzle of boiling pots and the rattle of busy kitchenware.

"He was a writer who wanted solitude but craved company," writes Niven, speculating that Wilder's relative chastity was a result of sublimation and reflected the repressions in his character. Niven also conjectures that Wilder's use of the detached observer, like the Stage Manager in *Our Town* and the priest Chremes in *The Woman of Andros*, reflected his own disinterest in intimate relationships. "Wilder was not only the product of an upbringing that left its intimidating mark on his emotional and sexual life, but . . .a cynic wary of intimacy, full of doubts about himself and distrust of others."

Where he seemed to have been most at ease, apart from in New England villages, was in the storied past of Europe. An indifferent student in college, he excelled in classical languages, with a special affinity for Latin. Both *The Cabala* and his hugely successful novel *The Ides of March* were based on Roman history. South America fascinated him, too. His Pulitzer-Prize-winning novel, *The Bridge of San Luis Rey*, took place in Peru. It was his first best-seller, number one on the charts for 1928. In fact, most of Wilder's succeeding novels and some of his plays were set in exotic places. Almost all of them enjoyed a wide readership and vast audiences, and they made him enormously rich.

Wilder was lucky enough never to fall into critical disfavor, like so many of his literary contemporaries. When you consider the see-saw careers of O'Neill, Miller, Williams, and Albee as playwrights or even of Hemingway and Fitzgerald as novelists, you can appreciate what a charmed life Wilder led as a writer. Nevertheless, he always regarded his own work with genuine humility. Referring to the wild praise that greeted *The Bridge on the Luis Rey*, he wrote to a publisher: "'*Greatest novel of the age*' is likely to antagonize really cultivated people rather than win them. Tolstoy and Hardy and Conrad haven't been dead so awfully long." To F. Scott Fitzgerald, who admired the book as well, Wilder wrote: "It is wonderful to be liked by you and to have been told so, for the self-confidence I have exhibited in my work I have never been able to extend to my person."

One can almost hear him saying, "my *humble* person"; his modesty regarding his own achievements approaches a condition that we were once allowed to call "Oriental." This, and his generosity toward the talents of others, made him a natural friend of actresses, for whom he expressed the warmest praise. Chief among these were Irene Worth, Ruth Gordon, and Katharine Cornell. Tallulah Bankhead was, as usual, a volatile temperament, but Gordon became a life-long confidante and proved to be ideal casting as Dolly Levi in *The Matchmaker*, for which she won a Tony. (Ruth Gordon at the time was attached to Jed Harris, whom she later exchanged for the more genial Garson Kanin.)

It was with Harris that Wilder had what seems to have been the only quarrel of his life. Jed Harris, at the time, was Broadway's leading director, a brilliant but extremely domineering and egotistical man who treated a playwright's text as if it were his private property. *Our Town* eventually proved a huge hit on Broadway, running for 336 performances, but getting there was quite a trip. Wilder and Harris fought over every element of production, from the lighting to the choice of Broadway theatre. (Wilder wanted a large barn, not a drawing room environment like the Henry Miller.) "Jed lost courage about my central intention," Wilder wrote to Woolcott, "and moved the production over to a different set of emphases." In a highly uncharacteristic show of resentment, he sent a warning letter to Hemingway, who was planning to have Harris direct his play *The Fifth Column*: "You've seen him now . . . vivid psychological realism and intelligence, devious intelligence. But maybe you don't know the rest: tormented, jealous egotism, latent hatred of all engaged in creative work, and so on. Use him for his great gifts . . . but don't presuppose a long and happy collaboration. I feel something like a piker to write such a letter as this." It was one of the few even faintly acerbic remarks to issue from his pen. (Another was his reference to T. S. Eliot as an elitist who "doesn't like people.")

Nevertheless, this incident represents one of the most interesting things in the biography because it reveals that buried beneath this man's courtesy, decency, generosity, and imperturbability was a passion that rarely entered his work but had the capacity to transform it.

Before Wilder died in 1975, he completed his last novel, the semi-autobiographical *Theophilus North*. It was named after his still-born twin brother, Theophilus, and also after himself. (North was a partial anagram for Thornton.) Theophilus is a rascal who functions as detective, shaman, actor, and magician, enjoying the kind of wild adventures, and the kind of untamed emotions, that Thornton rarely allowed himself. Niven believes that this unborn identical twin left his brother "a haunting legacy as well as a survivor's instinctive guilt." Could he also have left Wilder the stimulus for his double aesthetic and divided nature? Was Theophilus the furtive radical self Thornton always seemed to be pursuing through the corridors of his art, the redskin lurking in the shadows, capable of rubbing some color in his brother's paleface features?

(2012)

Mel Brooks's America: Puttin' on the Spritz

Mel Brooks may well be remembered as one of the most subversive comedians ever born in this country. He is certainly one of the most irreverent. Wry, manic, good natured, polymorphic in his interests, yet relentlessly Jewish in his style, Brooks has followed a path that says as much about our culture as any other American career. Born Melvin Kaminsky in Brooklyn, New York, in 1924, he evolved from schoolboy victim of neighborhood bullies to Borscht Belt tummler to stand-up comic before his breakout as one of the principal writers in the Max Liebman *Your Show of Shows* stable of writers for Sid Caesar. The other racehorses in this derby included such comic thoroughbreds as Carl Reiner, Woody Allen, Larry Gelbart, Louise Kallen, and Neil Simon, all commissioned to develop material for the first television show devoted almost entirely to Jewish-driven parody.

Having formed a close association with Carl Reiner, the two of them began improvising skits based on an imaginary superannuated character who had been witness to almost all of biblical and human history. They had come up with the act in Max Liebman's office and later began performing it for friends at parties. It was eventually to become the basis for a wildly popular record series, begun in 1961 (under persuasion by Steve Allen) and generically known as The 2,000 Year Old Man. And even later, it was turned into a wonderful animated film and an invaluable CD archive (called "The Complete History").

In that series, Brooks, always in close collaboration with the indispensable Carl Reiner, explored the comic tension between contemporary life and past history through his creation of an incredibly ancient Jew, an obvious impostor with his thick contemporary Yiddish-Brooklyn accent, whose memory goes back through the ages to investigate such historical landmarks as the beginnings of language ("Don't throw that rock."), the discovery of women in a cave ("Hey, I think there's ladies here."), the dating habits of Joan of Arc ("I went with her, dummy!"), and such revolutionary technological breakthroughs as Saran Wrap and Liquid Prell, all seen through a relentlessly Yiddish perspective.

It was inevitable, now that Brooks's gifts as a writer were being reinforced by his genius as a performer, that he would turn his attention from television and recording appearances to the Hollywood studio, where, as writer-director, occasional composer, and periodic supporting actor, he created eleven major motion pictures in twenty-seven years, followed by two major Broadway musicals.

Brooks's best films are satiric reflections on classic American movie genres, driven by his brilliantly parodic comic imagination. But Brooks's satire did not issue, full-blown, from the brain of some zany Semitic demigod. It came, rather, from a long tradition of Jewish comedy, with both Yiddish and American roots. Brooks's influences could be traced to Yiddish theatre, vaudeville, burlesque, popular comedy, and satire, as Jews began to feel secure enough in their adopted country to flaunt rather than hide their ethnic identity. This confidence came belatedly to the movies. Whereas studio heads (most of them also Jewish), like Harry Cohen and Jack and Harry Warner, once forced Jewish actors to change their names (like Paul Muni and John Garfield) or their noses (like Everett Sloane) or both (like Stella Adler/Ardler) in order to obtain choice movie roles, Hollywood was now permitting them to retain their own ethnicity and even to capitalize on it.

For this, Hollywood could largely thank Mel Brooks, who, like Venus rising full blown from a sea of Matzah ball soup, surfaced with a priceless capacity to turn everything terrestrial (and sometimes extra-terrestrial—consider *Space Balls*) into a Jewish joke. Thus, Brooks managed to Yiddishize some of the most revered Hollywood genres: *Blazing Saddles*, which stamped Hollywood Westerns like *Shane*, *Treasure of Sierra Madre*, and *True Grit* with a kosher imprint; *Young Frankenstein*, which satirized Universal Studio horror movies, at the same time parodying Fred Astaire and Ginger Rogers musicals like *Top Hat* and *Roberta* with its climactic "Puttin' on the Ritz" dance number featuring the Monster and the

Mad Doctor sporting canes and high hats; *Silent Movie*, performed entirely in silence, which paid a kind of delicatessen homage to Charlie Chaplin and Buster Keaton, the early acting heroes Brooks worshipped while living on Coney Island; *High Anxiety*, which sent up such darkling Hitchcock thrillers as *Notorious* and *North By Northwest*, and their impossibly involuted plots; The *History of the World: Part I*, which, in a whirlwind tour of the past, Yiddishized the whole of human history, not to mention the portentous biblical epics of Cecil B. DeMille (himself an unacknowledged Jew); *Space Balls*, which lampooned the sci-fi fantasies of Steven Spielberg (*Close Encounters of the Third Kind*) and George Lucas (*Star Wars*); *Life Stinks*, an urban comedy where he starred as a rich man trying to prove he could live on the streets of New York without any money; *Robin Hood: Men In Tights*, which caricatured the Hollywood costume epics immortalized by the likes of Errol Flynn and Olivia de Havilland; and *Dracula Dead and Living*, which brought Brooks back again to the realm of ethnicized horror movies.

But the Mel Brooks inheritance actually began shortly before he was born, in the early 1920s, when Yiddish humor was already having a powerful influence on American vaudeville and burlesque. Such venues eventually produced legendary comics like Smith and Dale, Bert Lahr, Bobby Clark, Phil Silvers, Shelley Berman, Zero Mostel, Milton Berle, and a host of other comic geniuses.

Burlesque comedy had been flourishing in New York in the twenties and thirties, until it was banned by Mayor LaGuardia because a chorine had forgotten to wear her G-string. As a result of this historical instance of benign neglect, burlesque was exiled to New Jersey. Wherever it appeared, however, burlesque theatre was dominated not just by nubile strippers but also by Jewish comedians, almost inevitably accompanied in their bawdy endeavors by one or two of the more well-endowed chorus girls—a few of which, like Gypsy Rose Lee, were Jewish, too.

The burlesque skit entertained the spectator both with fleshly arousal and comic shtick, as it had since the time of Aristophanes. There is a scene in Neil Simon's *The Sunshine Boys* that essentializes this double function, when a scantily-dressed, amply-bosomed nurse sashays into the consulting room of a doctor (played by Walter Matthau): "Nursey, nursey," he says in a leering rebuke to her, "why are you busting in here?"

The centerpiece of *The Sunshine Boys*, the doctor skit, was based on the immortal Doctor Kronkheit sketch of Smith and Dale. But the training grounds for countless Jewish entertainers was not just Minsky's strip joints or the vaudeville circuit but also the Borscht Belt, including such sadly defunct Catskill entertainment centers as Grossinger's, the Concord, the Delmar, and (in the Poconos of Pennsylvania) Tamiment.

Most of the burlesque and vaudeville graduates eventually went from marginal show biz forms into mainstream "legitimate" American entertainment during the major part of the twentieth century, where their names became known far beyond the walls of grind houses. After studying violin and touring the vaudeville circuit, for example, that great master of comic timing from Waukegan, Illinois, Benjamin Kubelsky, changed his name to Jack Benny and originated the legendary *Jack Benny Show* on radio and TV. He also married Sadie Marx, a cousin of the Marx Brothers, who later changed her name to Mary Livingstone. And on radio and TV, Gertrude Edelstein Berg originated and starred in *The Goldbergs* around the same time that Ethel Merman (born Ethel Agnes Zimmerman) and Sophie Tucker (born Sonya Kalish) were preparing the way for a long line of Jewish belters, culminating in Barbra Streisand, their uncrowned successor, and one of the few Jewish performers who refused to change her name, or nose, for Hollywood (aside from dropping the second "a" in Barbara).

The theatre, of course, was always particularly partial to Jewish material, even after television began to steal its thunder in the 1950s. Yet, even in the early days of Hollywood, Jewish acid somehow managed to seep into the homogenized milk.

The vaudeville team of Groucho, Harpo, Chico, and Zeppo Marx (known as Minnie's Boys) left the New York vaudeville circuit to bring their riotous anarchy to Paramount Studios where they revolutionized Hollywood farce. Minnie's Boys were a family of closely knit Jewish brothers, who made their fraternal scratchiness almost an element of their style, and so did their Jewish family imitators, the Ritz Brothers, and the Three Stooges: Moe, Larry, and Shemp Howard.

An even earlier exception to Hollywood foreskin replacement was the budding cantor-turned-teaterzinger in *The Jolson Story* played by Al Jolson (born Asa Yoelson). Another was Groucho Marx as Captain Spalding in *Animal Crackers*, blowing cigar smoke into people's eyes while rolling his own and singing "My name is Captain Spalding, the African explorer," ("Did someone call me schnorrer?") With this musical aside, Groucho smuggled into *Animal Crackers* one of the first Yiddish phrases ever to emanate from a Hollywood studio.

Indeed, despite Groucho's shambling gait, diagonal stance, and painted vaudeville mustache; despite Chico's exaggerated Italian accent, checked pants, and bow tie; and despite Harpo's blond wig, top hat and lubricious leer, the hard-edged unromantic satire of the Marx Brothers (Zeppo excluded—he was always meant to be the all-American love interest) remained unmistakably Jewish throughout all of their movies, including *Duck Soup*, where they imported an old ethnic vaudeville routine—"Flywheel, Shyster, and Flywheel"—into the picture virtually intact.

Perhaps as a mechanism of defense, Jews managed to monopolize American comedy—at least until the coming of such great African-American standups as Richard Pryor, Eddie Murphy, and Chris Rock. On the television screen, in early years, the appearance of Jews was almost as rare as in the movies. But soon, that great vaudeville schlamazel, Phil Silvers, was to transform himself into the wily Sergeant Bilko, a paradigm of the Jewish make-out artist.

Another vaudeville legend, Milton Berle, became the fast-talking compere of the *Texaco Star Theatre*, a version of the Jewish con man, selling goods off a pushcart. The great Lenny Bruce sacrificed his brilliant nightclub career on the altar of free expletive expression. And of course, the inimitable Sid Caesar, Mel Brooks's exacting patron, having graduated from a Catskill comic into a major TV star, was impersonating countless ethnic characters on Max Liebman's *Your Show of Shows*, while his inspired stable of idea men were evolving into sought-after Hollywood movie writers, accomplished Broadway playwrights, and brilliant stage and screen directors.

Based on his recordings, his eleven cinematic adventures, and his two Broadway musicals—not to mention the remake of *To Be Or Not To Be* he made with his beloved wife and (until her untimely death in 2005) creative inspiration, Anne Bancroft—Brooks may have been the most shameless and endearing Jewish comic of them all. Just consider the range of characters on the *2000 Year Old Man* recording, which includes a priceless track called "The Two Hour Old Baby," in which Brooks plays an infant born with complete control of language and feelings of nostalgia for his lost umbilical cord. (He intends to replace it with a key chain.) I had the good fortune to be present at one of those early recording sessions where I heard a skit (dropped from the record) about a CPA who tells a wealthy client who is trying to evade income taxes to live under the Yangtze River and breathe through a straw!

Actually, beginning with his first full-length feature, *The Producers*, Mel Brooks turned from being the disembodied voice of an incredibly ancient Jew into the channel for a large gallery of manic American con men. The form of *The Producers* is that of Hollywood's typical Broadway success story like that immortalized in *42nd Street*. ("You're going out a youngster, but you've got to come back a star.") But *The Producers* is hardly an inspirational show biz tribute. From the opening moment of this riotous film, it is obvious that we're not in Kansas anymore. Following a shadow play of frenzied lovemaking glimpsed through the smoky window of a producer's office, the door opens to reveal not Clark Gable and Ava Gardner locked in amorous embrace but the enormous sum of Zero Mostel (born Samuel Joel Mostel), bulging in a red smoking jacket, his patented strands of hair plastered over his forehead like seaweed on a rock. He is wooing one of his octogenarian female backers ("Do you have the little checkie?") with his customary blend of predatory charm and unconstrained ferocity. Not to mention transformative grace—he can turn himself into a purring cat with the same astonishing ease that a few years later on Broadway he will manage to change himself into Ionesco's *Rhinoceros*.

No, we're not in Kansas with Dorothy and Toto; we're in the Catskills with Sid Caesar and Carl Reiner, where Brooks cut his comic eye teeth. Why else name your hero (Max Bialystock) after an item from a Jewish bakery and the Polish shtetl that originated it? And why make Bialystock's nervous wreck of a partner—the neurasthenic CPA, Leo Bloom (played by Gene Wilder, born Jerome Silberman)—a namesake of James Joyce's Jewish wanderer in *Ulysses*?

Hysterically performed by the blue-eyed, curly-headed Wilder as a regressive infant groping a blue blankie, Leo Bloom is a hissy-fit Faust corrupted by a Shubert Alley Mephistopheles who has wrested from him the secret of if not of eternal life, then of unlimited capital gains: producing the worst musical in history, closing it fast, and banking the production money. In the climactic seduction scene, Bialystock wins Bloom's soul by infantalizing him with colored balloons, merry-go-round rides, and a boat trip in Central Park: "I'm happy," shrieks the delirious accountant.

We are happy too, and in the scenes that follow, Brooks delights us further with characters like the Nazi playwright Franz Liebkind (Kenneth Mars, whose incomparable Kraut accent will be rehabilitated later when he plays the Police Chief in *Young Frankenstein*); the transvestite director Roger De Bris (Christopher Hewitt) and his campy aide-de-camp Carmen Ghia (Andreas Voutsinas); and Dick Shawn as a hippy Hitler in a musical so tasteless that it freezes the audience into an oil painting of paralyzed horror. (Later, Mel Brooks would swell his growing repertory company of comic actors with comedians borrowed from such variety vaudevilles as *Caesar's Hour* and *The Carol Burnett Show*, notably Harvey Korman and Tim Conway and such reigning comic actors as Cloris Leachman and Madeline Kahn.)

As in its later Broadway musical reincarnation, the movie of *The Producers* manages to offend virtually everybody: Jews, Germans, gays, radical feminists, handicapped old ladies, even the table manners of actors. ("Have you ever eaten with one?") Brooks will get to African-Americans a few years later in *Blazing Saddles*. But his main target in *The Producers* is Hitler's Third Reich, reduced to a routine featuring buxom chorines in Wagnerian headdresses and black-shirted storm-troopers goose-stepping in a manner that would have brought joy to the heart of Busby Berkeley.

In both its Hollywood and Broadway musical manifestations, the Waffen-SS, for example, are transformed into a coven of show biz chorus boys. ("Don't be stupid; Be a smarty. Come and join the Nazi party," they sing in "Springtime for Hitler," reportedly composed by Brooks himself and the original title for the movie.) It is an inspired moment that has anointed Brooks as the Jew who killed Hitler by impaling him on the spike of remorseless satire.

There is a girly show in the movie of *The Producers* called "War and Piece." Later, when he turns the film into a Broadway musical, Brooks will improve and Judaize his weakness for bad puns with the theatre posters on Bialystock's wall: *This Too Shall Pass, The Breaking Wind, A Streetcar Named Murray, She Shtups to Conquer, Katz,* and *High Button Jews.* There are, no doubt, similar posters sitting on the walls of Mel Brooks's own office, commemorating his memorable career as a Hollywood producer-director-writer-composer-star. They are posters that are engraved in our memories, and they have made Melvin Kaminsky immortal.

(2012)

The Like Generation

In the 1960s and '70s, young people were referred to as the "Love Generation," partly because of their insistence on sexual freedom, which they proposed as an alternative ("Make love, not war.") to the Vietnam conflict. Today's young people could be more accurately identified as the "Like Generation," for reasons that I will now attempt to describe.

The most immediate one has to do with their repetitive, ritualistic use of the word "like." I defy you to listen to more than two or three sentences by any contemporary twenty- or thirty-year-old without hearing that term repeated like a mantra. "It was-like-the best experience of my life." "I was driving-like-down Route 95." "I had this-like-terrific pain in my gut." "I guzzled-like-three dark Coronas in a row." "We have an apartment-like-in Belvedere Towers." Even when young people are being precise about numbers or addresses, they feel compelled to employ this increasingly boring monosyllable.

Properly used, the word "like" is an essential component of simile. "I feel like a lonesome child." "Taking that river trip was like floating down the Nile." The one thing may not be identical to the other, but it is very *like* it. Unfortunately, however, it is not as a simile or a comparison that "like" is being used today. The apartment is not like a pad in the Belvedere Towers; it is a pad in the Belvedere Towers. You weren't driving down a highway that looked like Route 95; you were on Route 95. Using the word in this contemporary fashion is the same as using the phrase "you know." It is a momentary interruptive that allows you time to think of the appropriate term.

The repetition of "like" by an entire generation, however, also suggests that the group is dominated not just by imprecision, but by lukewarm caution. Having taught both generations, I believe I can generalize with some authority: The Love Generation was passionate, inflamed, and engaged. The Like Generation is prudent, ambitious, and escapist. The first would shut down a university and occupy a dean's office to protest an unjust war—admittedly while ignoring the munitions factory right up the street. The second is largely absorbed with such private obsessions as tweeting and video games and is only truly exercised by things that might affect their careers. (Admittedly, life is much more frightening in a time of economic blight than during war-time prosperity.) When one of my students, for example, asks a question these days, it is usually not about the text under discussion, but rather about his grade. He needs an A- rather than a B+ to get into law or business school.

I'm not arguing that the sometimes uncivil behavior of the Love Generation is preferable to the more gentle deportment of their modern counterparts—only that passivity is having a poisonous effect on our politics. The Love Generation used to riot over any perceived ideological slight. The Like

Generation—in the face of the most outrageous and obstructionist behavior in memory on the part of Washington legislators, Wall Street bankers, and the NRA—is raising no strong protests or showing any significant resistance to what their elders are doing to the country. Polls tell us that almost 90 percent of Americans favor some form of gun control. Yet today, when schoolchildren are being slaughtered by assault weapons and when Congress persistently refuses to pass even the most listless law (such as background checks) to rectify the situation, does anyone take to the streets? No, as Yeats noted, it is the worst who are full of passionate intensity, while the best lack all conviction.

Yes, I know, there is Occupy Wall Street. But what are its goals? Have they ever been properly articulated? Are they having any effect? The very inchoateness of the Occupy Movement suggests that it has not yet formulated a coherent and plausible protest. Barack Obama is currently being blamed, particularly by Maureen Dowd (wrongly I believe), for failing to exercise strong leadership and get his legislation passed, as FDR pushed through the New Deal and LBJ the Great Society. But Obama is stuck with an implacable Republican majority in the House, and you can't twist arms when there are sharp razors up your opponents' sleeves, not to mention flabby muscle groups in those of your own party. How would you like to spend your days in office looking into the hostile faces of Lindsey Graham, John Boehner, or Mitch McConnell?

This is not an occasion to rail against our paralyzed nonfunctioning government. I'd rather try to arouse the people who elected it. How can even the strongest president handle such an inflexible opposition party without the backing of an outraged electorate? Silent citizens allow wealthy contributors to call the shots. It's clear enough what produced the Tea Party: a racist, selfish reactionary class of rich and would-be rich, eager to destroy anyone who doesn't protect low taxes and high profits. But it is the Like Generation that must take some of the blame for the general wobbliness of such Democrats as Harry Reid. (Yes, he is finally standing up to the opposition and trying to drive home the bills required to repair a broken nation.) What the electorate lacks since the disappearance of socialist theory is a persuasive left-wing ideology that might serve as a spur to progressive legislative action, as workers pushed back in the thirties and students in the sixties. Without this-you know?-we will continue to be-like-adrift in our own backyards.

(2013)

Return of the Booboisie

"Absolute reason expired at eleven o'clock last night," a character shouts in the mad scene from Ibsen's *Peer Gynt*. That certainly seems to describe the mental condition of present-day America. A group of lunatics have shut down the United States government because they don't like a health bill already approved by both houses of Congress and sanctioned by the Supreme Court.

Everyone is puzzling over how a small minority of fanatics has managed to exercise such power over the entire Republican Party, not to mention the nation as a whole. But from the grim look on John Boehner's straight face every time he emerges from a meeting to make a statement, the Tea Party clearly feels it has been authorized to do a lot of harm to anyone who crosses it.

And what accounts for this extraordinary confidence? Granting justified complaints about gerrymandering, the Tea Party nevertheless has the backing of a significant number of people in this country. Certainly, new voting laws have delivered electoral power over to people who otherwise would have less voice in deciding its fate. But I don't think that is the whole story. From the relative absence of national outrage (apart from Democratic fundraisers) over this usurpation of power and how it has been injuring our country in the last few weeks, one has to conclude that vast numbers of Americans have either become indifferent to the fate of their nation or fail to understand the enormity of the crisis.

H. L. Mencken used to rail again what he called the "boobcracy" of America, meaning a system accountable to majorities with little culture, humanity, or intelligence. I think it is time to haul this phrase out of the attic where it has been collecting dust for the past seventy years or so and apply it to our current political condition. We are still a nation of boobs, and the boobs we have elected to lead us into a totally unnecessary government shutdown are a perfect example of how a failure of education and culture can turn a democracy into a boobocracy.

(2013)

China Begins to Dream

Last May, my wife and I travelled to China in order to spend two weeks at the International Theatre Festival in Wuzhen. I had recently been appointed Honorary Chairman of the event, which also included among its six presentations the final play in my Shakespeare Trilogy. The Festival's initial year was 2013, and for the occasion a philanthropic businessman with advanced architectural tastes named Chen Xianghong had funded a state-of-the-art 1,100-seat glass and filigree theatre called the Grand, as well as subsidizing the renovation of four additional facilities. Although Mr. Chen is a former Communist official, there was little government involvement in the project apart from stamping it approved.

Wuzhen is a picturesque theme park on a Venice-like canal, which draws about six million tourists a year. It has lively store fronts that display such ancient Chinese practices as silk-work weaving and foot-binding. It also boasts very clean air and a number of elegant four-star hotels with luxurious accommodations, healthy food, and immaculate service. You cannot drop a pea pod or a crumb of bread without it instantly being whisked up by a vigilant domestic and deposited in a plastic bag.

If this sounds different than the China we've been hearing about from the media, with its contaminated chickens, floating pigs, poisoned air, corruption, cyber espionage, human rights abuse, child control, inhumane prison treatment, and, most recently, rural relocation, well it is. The Festival leaders were obviously more interested in turning a different face to the world, particularly to show their pride in Chinese theatre artists—not to mention their curiosity about American and European cultures. Western food was plentiful and satisfying. And while virtually nobody in our group knew a word of Chinese besides "Thank you" and "Hello," a lot of Chinese spoke flawless English. True, the local plays we saw were hardly activist. The only political criticism to be heard was at least half a century old, directed against the Japanese in World War II and Mao's Cultural Revolution in the sixties.

Still, there was no sign of fear in the people in Wuzhen, no trace of anxiety in the eyes of the tourists or the faces of the audiences, perhaps demonstrating the capacity of a strong national spirit to survive political repression, at least within reason. Anticipating the warming political relations between the newly-elected Chinese president, Xi Jinping, and President Obama, the Festival's cultural atmosphere was permeated with friendship, cooperation, and courtesy by the Chinese toward Westerners, accompanied by an almost frantic eagerness on the part of young girls to get your photograph on their iPhones—preferably with your arms around their shoulders. The smiling faces you passed in the street formed a striking contrast with the often curdled expressions of our countrymen back home, just as their placid strolling is an implicit rebuke to our native road rage.

Wuzhen has ambitions to become a major international event and, judging from its first season, it will almost certainly realize them. The initial program featured a mix of six productions equally divided between East and West, plus panels, street mimes, carnivals, and lively student competitions. Coming from Europe was *Inside the Skeleton of the Whale*, a piece conceived by the Grotowski disciple Eugenio Barba and his Danish Odin Teatret company. Invited from the United States were David Henry Hwang's *The Dance and the Railroad* from the Signature Theatre and my own *The Last Will* from the Abingdon Theatre. Coming from China were three productions, which constituted the most significant—and, surprisingly, most experimental—works of the Festival.

One was a crime story set to a rock score called *About the Murder of Hanging Garden* and directed by the avant-garde artist Meng Jinghui. Another was *The Yellow Storm*, centering on the Japanese invasion of Beijing in 1937, written, staged, and designed by the triple-threat woman auteur, Tian Qinxin (whose *Green Snake* is scheduled to be produced at the Kennedy Center).

But the most awe-inspiring Asian entry was *A Dream Like a Dream*, an eight-hour epic by the extraordinary theatre artist (and Festival Artistic Director) Stan Lai, also known as Lai Sheng-Chuan, whom the BBC has called "probably the best Chinese language director and playwright in the world."

As for *A Dream Like a Dream*, which Lai has been working on since the year 2000, it in turn has been hailed by the leading Chinese critic, Raymond Zhou, as not only Lai's finest play, but as "a major milestone in Chinese theatre, possibly the greatest Chinese play since time immemorial." I don't have the knowledge to confirm this judgment. But it seems less extravagant when you realize that modern Chinese playwriting is a relatively new phenomenon. (There were plays written for a while under the old dynasties but until the early part of the twentieth century, theatre in China was mostly composed of Beijing and Cantonese opera and shadow puppetry).

Still, such hyperbolic praise is especially impressive given the fact that Lai, who has written over thirty full-length plays, is not Chinese but Taiwanese. He was born and raised, in fact, in the United States until the age of twelve during the period in which his father was serving as a diplomat in Washington. (Lai later returned to this country with his wife Nai-chu Ding to earn a PhD degree from UC-Berkeley.) And, as if to confirm the unusual intercontinental reach of Lai's writing, the first workshop of his latest play was actually done in 2000 at Berkeley, and in English.

Clearly, the traditional tensions between Taiwan and China no longer seem to exist. Lai's work travels freely between the two countries and cultures. Before *A Dream Like a Dream*, the most celebrated theatre piece by this playwright was *Secret Love for the Peach Blossom Spring* (1986), which his wife produced six years later as a movie in Taiwan. *Secret Love* is a Pirandello-like double play that combines written text with actors' rehearsals and improvisations for the purpose of breaking down the barriers between stage and reality. It displays an unusual capacity to meld the past and the present, both in story and technique, so that medieval history is being dramatized side by side with a contemporary plot.

A Dream Like a Dream, which also combines modern events and past history, was partially created by Lai's Performance Theatre out of "crosstalk" (or *xiangsheng*, the Chinese word for standup comedy). The playwright provides the outline, the actors extemporize on it, and then the playwright edits the results. America, of course, can boast an outstanding tradition of improvised standup, from Lenny Bruce to Lewis

Black to Louis C. K. Less impressive is the improvisational technique encouraged, say, by our method school of acting, where actors often explore their own personalities instead of the ones they are being paid to play.

By contrast, Chinese performers possess a kind of humility not often seen in our celebrity culture, though one can see plenty of simulations in Academy and Tony Award acceptance speeches. Huang Lei, the founding director of the Festival and the man who first conceived it, though a wildly popular film and TV star in China, not only sought a relatively small part in one of the Festival plays, but also manages a bar in Wuzhen that you reach by walking through his home! Imagine visiting Arnold Schwarzenegger's Santa Monica bistro, Schatzi on Main, through his kitchen.

Later, I learned, with agreeable surprise, that the leading grey-haired old lady in Stan Lai's play was actually a well-known (and ravishingly beautiful) and youngish movie star. American celebrities willing to submerge their egos in a character part are considerably rarer; Meryl Streep is one of a few such transforming artists—most recently playing Margaret Thatcher in *The Iron Lady*. And Stella Adler famously (albeit peevishly) aged up in the thirties to take on the role of Bessie Berger, the mother in Clifford Odets's *Awake and Sing*. But this kind of self-effacement seems to be a trademark rather than an exception in the Chinese theatre. At the risk of overgeneralizing, I suggest that the capacity for transformation personified even among even the greatest stars in China can be attributed to distinctive qualities in the Chinese character, notably unusual modesty and a singular shortage of egotism.

As the title of *A Dream Like a Dream* suggests, the play belongs to an honorable category of works that perhaps began with Shakespeare's *A Midsummer Night's Dream*, before being developed by Pedro Calderón de la Barca in *Life is a Dream* and August Strindberg in *A Dream Play*. (It was later systematized in the contemporary theatrical form known as Expressionism.) Lai's dream play has its religious roots in Buddhism, and its breakdown of time and space creates a kind of fractured reality that embodies the spirit of Zen. In his excellent article about the Festival published in *Salon.com*, the critic Jonathan Kalb accurately describes the play as "a structure of Chinese boxes, stories, and dreams within other stories and dreams."

The only Western theatre pieces I know to match the eight-hour length of *A Dream Like a Dream* are the RSC's eight-and-one-half hour *Nicholas Nickleby*, Peter Brooks's nine-hour *Mahabharata*, and *KA MOUNTain and GUARDenia Terrace*, Robert Wilson's week-long marathon atop a mountain in Iran. The duration of Lai's play is not only explained by the fact that it covers almost seventy years of human history, beginning in 1933 and ending in the year of the new millennium. It also follows the life experiences of at least three principal characters, played by two or three actors each, so that a character not only moves through time by aging but also through space by appearing in two places at the same time.

All three characters are sick, and all three are preparing to die. Dying (along with traveling) is, in fact, the central metaphor of the play, which, cycling through the decades, takes extinction and regeneration as its ultimate destinations. The audience is arranged on swivel seats, around which the thirty-two actors parade clockwise, sometimes carrying briefcases, at varying speeds on specially-constructed ramps above their heads, while the settings change frequently to accommodate the multiple scenes. The result is a sense of accelerated bustle, rather like being in Grand Central Station while three trains are taking on passengers simultaneously.

The dream-death metaphor is established in the very first moment with an account of the fictional pre-Han Dynasty poet, Zhuang Heng, an invention of the playwright, being imprisoned by a Chinese emperor who, like Mao during the Cultural Revolution, is preparing to imprison or exterminate all the scholars and artists in order to rewrite human history. (The parallels to Mao are not accidental.) Zhuang escapes this fate by imagining a magnificent world for himself near a lake that he fully enters on the day of his execution. He leaves behind a poem called an "Ode Like a Dream" with the following verse:

> This floating life is like a dream
> But if a dream is not a dream, What then is this floating life?
> A dream like a dream.

Echoing not only the name of his play but that of Calderón's, Stan Lai then proceeds to embroider his own dream. For this purpose, he has woven together his three other dream stories, each revolving around a diseased, or potentially diseased, individual. The first features a character named Doctor A—played by an actor who also plays Doctor B. She is depressed by the callousness and cynicism of her profession and by the death of her patients until she meets Patient #5A—also played by an actor called Patient #5B—who is being treated for an undiagnosed disease. Later, we follow Patient #5A to Paris, where he becomes involved with a Chinese waitress and where he then encounters a mysterious old lady named Koo, with whom he acts out the third story.

In the second story, we follow the journey of a younger Koo—played by yet another ravishing actress—once a desirable prostitute in a brothel, pursued by many men. Among these is a lovesick French consul, the aristocratic Henri. Henri marries Koo, after divorcing his present wife, and takes her first to Paris, then to his château in Normandy, a magical place where, it is said, you can sometimes see your own image in a lake, like the poet Zhuang did at the beginning of the play. After getting erotically involved with a number of avant-garde artists (including a zany surrealist named Salvador!), Koo herself begins to paint.

Count Henri seems to regard her extramarital affairs with chilly forbearance, until one day he leaves Paris on a train and never returns. Koo believes him to be dead, since the train blew up leaving the station and there is no other trace of him than his suitcase. When she goes to withdraw some cash from the bank, Koo discovers that Henri has already closed the account, and all of her paintings in the safe deposit box have disappeared, except for one of herself and the Count on the wall of their now foreclosed Normandy estate.

Many years later, Henri reappears, as the husband of a rich African woman for whom Koo is working as a maid. Paralyzed by surprise, she leaves the house without confronting her former husband. But the revenge she later takes is worth the wait.

The third story centers on Koo as an old lady, now confined to a wheelchair and being tended by Patient #5B. In this story the various strands of the play are interwoven like the fabric of a multicolored nomadic tapestry until they become virtually seamless in their pattern of unity.

Although somewhat marred toward the end by some uncharacteristically homiletic passages, *A Dream Like a Dream*, is, I believe, the masterpiece critics claim it to be. And the scope and ambition of the play suggests a genuine resurgence in Chinese-language drama and audience appetite for it, just as our own is flagging and drooping. Imagine a popular nonmusical play on Broadway testing your concentration for eight hours instead of the customary eighty minutes. Imagine an audience that responds to the most experimental work with those teenage squeals usually reserved for rock stars. Imagine tickets to an experimental avant-garde exercise such as *A Dream Like a Dream* being sold for more money (over one thousand dollars) than scalped seats to *The Book of Mormon*!

Imagine thirty-two actors on an American stage today for any presentation other than a blockbuster musical comedy. (As a matter of fact, Stan Lai is currently writing the book for a Broadway musical based on the martial arts expert Bruce Lee. It will be interesting to see how well the commercial American and Chinese experimental theatre cultures intersect!)

This season in New York, in addition to the usual musicals, we have had a one-man *Macbeth* and a one-woman *Medea*, an off-Broadway menu limited to three actors per play, and a Broadway audience composed almost entirely of middle-aged women with sleeping husbands, out-of-town tourists, and corporate executives wooing potential buyers on an expense account. Some of this disparity can be attributed to the fact that China's huge population (1.35 billion) is almost four times the size of our own. But it is also doubtless due to the unchecked energy that is bubbling out of this fascinating and contradictory country. China's audience is young; ours is superannuated. China looks to the unknown future while we revive our familiar past. Maybe Chinese plays can teach us something about how to rejuvenate a faltering, doddering, senescent theatre and restore it to life. *A Dream Like a Dream*, along with other productions coming from China, could very well revive our faith in the belief that art has a lot more power than the state to elevate our spirits and improve our lives.

(2013)

Note

1. After a disastrous off-Broadway run in 1970 directed by Carmen Capalbo and starring Barbara Harris and Estelle Parsons, the Yale Repertory Theatre did a full-orchestra production of *Mahagonny* in 1974, in a translation by Michael Feingold that persuaded Lenya to let us do the highly successful American premiere of a show she had previously banned, *Happy End* (in 1975), which led to its 1977 Broadway premiere with former Yale company members Christopher Lloyd and Meryl Streep.

2

Playwright Passages

Aeschylus

Aeschylus is the first Western playwright whose work has come down to us in more than fragments. He began writing tragedy twenty-five hundred years ago, just a year after the beginning of the fifth century BC, and of his seventy or more plays, only seven survive in relatively complete form. Yet, this remote Athenian giant has remained one of the most powerful and influential playwrights who ever lived.

Aeschylus's plays—like those of his contemporaries and followers—are all based on Homeric myths. In this, Greek tragedy most resembles the Christian medieval cycles that were also dependent on sacred texts. (The cycle plays started with the Creation and ended with the Harrowing of Hell.) But the more sophisticated European drama that followed the mystery plays mostly rejected Biblical material, finding inspiration in secular stories. The body of Greek tragedy, on the other hand, never abandoned its hieratic roots. It formed a continuing series of variations on the same myths seen from different points of view; see for example the way that Aeschylus, Sophocles, and Euripides each handled the recognition scene between Electra and Orestes.

The one trilogy Aeschylus wrote—indeed the only extant Greek trilogy (though it lacks a requisite satyr play)—is his *Oresteia*. All of the playwright's strengths are evident in these plays—his pious, dense, and obscure style; his patriotic passion for his country and his interest in its evolving legal system; and his sense that humans are subject to celestial oversight. In the scope and ambition of his work, Aeschylus will not only influence his Greek successors. He will also function as a model for the drama to come, especially in nineteenth-century Germany and twentieth-century Europe and America.

Eugene O'Neill's monumental trilogy *Mourning Becomes Electra*, for example, owes a huge debt to the *Oresteia*, as does Jean-Paul Sartre's *Les Mouches* (*The Flies*), and T. S. Eliot's *The Family Reunion*. Although Western dramatists still remain rather reluctant to turn over Biblical soil, they have shown no hesitation in tilling the Homeric myths of Greek drama. And it is Aeschylus, rather than the more modern Sophocles or skeptical Euripides, who has remained their primary model, adapted for modern purposes. In 1966, for example, Robert Lowell wrote a version of Aeschylus's *Prometheus Bound* that served as a fierce condemnation of the Vietnam War.

The reason for Aeschylus's continuing influence on modern drama, I believe, is his passionate concern for the polis and his dedicated patriotic fervor. He wrote *The Persians* after having actually participated in the Persian Wars. He designed *Seven Against Thebes* as a fierce condemnation of civil strife. He conceived *The Suppliants* as a plea for women in choosing their own mates. And in the last play of his *Oresteia*, namely *The Eumenides*, he fashioned a theatrical metaphor for the founding of the Athenian justice system. In this play, pursued by the Furies, Orestes is brought before the court of the Areopagus for the murder of his mother. And when Athena chooses to resolve human conflict through law rather than tribal revenge, Orestes is arraigned, in the first trial in history, before a jury of his peers. Typically, the jury is hung, and Athena casts the deciding vote for Orestes on the premise that the mother is not the true parent of the child.

Although properly outraged by this bizarre decision, the Furies are finally persuaded by Athena to transform into the more benign Eumenides, and let the courts rather than tribal vengeance decide on future criminal issues. As an isolated legal decision, Athena's patriarchal prejudices are hardly designed to endear her to modern readers. But the scene represents a major step in the progress of civilization: the creation of an organized legal system within a tragic play. Aeschylus emerges from *The Oresteia*, as he does from his other six extant works, not only as a great poet and dramatist, but as a great patriot, a great peacemaker, and a great civic philosopher.

(2010)

Edward Albee

As the unwanted and often renegade adopted son of two wealthy Westchester conservatives, Edward Albee has always displayed a strong ambivalence in his character and his work. Indeed, the conflict between the seemingly placid world of convention and the uncontrollable forces boiling beneath the surface of society may someday be seen as the continuing tension of his plays. If we are to believe the playwright, Albee's adoptive parents were like Ibsen's Pillars of Society—outwardly respectable, inwardly contemptible. As a high school dropout, a dedicated alcoholic, and a gay man—and as one who sympathized deeply with the oppressed of the world—Albee seemed to find his very definition in the conflict between the suburban square and the Bohemian hipster.

From the moment Peter confronts Jerry on a village park bench in *The Zoo Story*—Albee's first American success—this conflict is clear. If Jerry at first seems to be the menace, it is Peter who proves to be the (unwitting) murderer. Jerry impales himself on the knife he places in Peter's hand, thus forcing him to confront the demon living below his respectable skin.

It would be wrong, however, to assume that Albee is simply satirizing the shopping mall world of convention. He is a product both of Suburbia and Bohemia, and his ineffectual efforts to resolve these warring elements within himself often provide the basic conflicts of his plays. Take one of his masterpieces, *Who's Afraid of Virginia Woolf?*, for example. George and Martha are presumably named after the father of our country and his wife. But instead of representing a united front of patriotism and respectability, this couple is embroiled in one of the most tumultuous marital strifes in all dramatic literature.

Or perhaps that distinction should be reserved for that earlier curdled relationship between Agamemnon and Clytemnestra in *The Oresteia* or between Adolph and Laura in *The Father* because, unlike Aeschylus and Strindberg, Albee shows us the genuine bond of love beneath the searing sexual hatred.

In this play, as in much of Albee's work, there is an element of prestidigitation and often a note of mischief. George aims a shotgun at his wife that transforms into a Japanese parasol. Martha rhapsodizes about a child who proves to be wholly imaginary. Unlike Arthur Miller, who believed that the world of absurd theatre threatened the reality of the family play, Albee was among the first (along with Ionesco in *The Bald Soprano*) to demonstrate that absurdity was very likely a crucial element of the domestic scene. This was a continuing theme in *A Delicate Balance* and *Everything in the Garden*, where Albee seemed to have momentarily abandoned his redskin attack on fortress America to become a paleface comedian of manners. And it reached some kind of climax in his writing of *The Goat, or Who Is Sylvia?* where the hero, a happily married family man with a gay son, falls passionately in love with a farmyard animal.

But perhaps the finest example of the wedding of Suburbia and Bohemia in Albee, the most poignant revelation of how rebellion can be leavened with the yeast of love, is to be found in his later play, *Three Tall Women.* There, Albee, in the character of a gay returning son, forgives his dying mother for all her trespasses—her meanness, her parsimony, her rejections, and her unloving nature. And instead of being impaled on the knife of respectability, as was Jerry in *The Zoo Story,* the son emerges from the experience a wiser, kinder, and more understanding human being.

Biographers have told us about the schizoid split in Albee's nature, depending on whether he was sober or drunk. That is another example of the rift in his nature between the good boy and the demon, the family man and the sexual desperado, the spirit that affirms and the spirit that denies. However much unhappiness these conflicts have caused him in his personal life, they are the stuff out of which great drama has been made.

(2010)

Aristophanes

Aristophanes, who wrote his plays between the last half of the fourth century BC and the first part of the third, is the oldest comic dramatist known to history. He is also one of the very best. Writing for a theatre dominated by such heroic playwrights as Aeschylus, Sophocles, and Euripides, Aristophanes was absolutely relentless in satirizing their tragic subjects and their tragic forms and absolutely fearless in lampooning many of the most respected religious, political, philosophical, and artistic figures of his day.

Though Aristophanes was a passionate pacifist, he was far from a radical firebrand. He was, rather, essentially a conservative thinker. True, he nagged at warmongers such as King Cleon for preventing an honorable resolution with Sparta. (Like some American hardliners, Cleon questioned the patriotism of anyone who proposed a negotiated peace.) But Aristophanes also took aim at such liberal sophists as Socrates for his Cloud Cuckoo-Land thinking and Euripides for his presumed misogyny. Neither was Aristophanes very tolerant toward contemporary gay relationships.

But the issue that most powerfully motivated Aristophanes was the endless Peloponnesian War, and a large part of his writing consisted of desperate fantasies about how to the end the hostilities. In this regard, his plays often had the quality of wishful dreams. In *Peace*, for instance, the play ends with a nude courtesan, named Peace, being pulled out of a pit and paraded around the city. For Aristophanes, eroticism represents the very opposite of war. The same kind of daydream animates *Lysistrata*, where a passionate housewife persuades the women of Athens and Sparta to withhold erotic favors from their husbands until the men agree to end the war. It is significant that all of Aristophanes's male characters are equipped with an enormous fabricated erection known as the phallos. In *Lyisistrata*, for obvious reasons, deprivation makes their erections particularly large. In a musical version of the play performed at the American Repertory Theatre in 2001, the phalluses were represented as colored balloons. At the end of the show, following an outbreak of peace, the women took their needles and burst them.

Much of Aristophanes's comedy is based on the contradiction between high spiritual aspirations and low physical functions. Indeed, this kind of functional comedy would later become the basis for much Western burlesque and farce. I'm not referring to the witty, often chaste banter between men and women in the act of courtship, but rather the raunchier, raucous comedy found in the low characters of Shakespeare. In the first part of the twentieth century in America, Minsky burlesques—named after the Minsky brothers—embodied a similar outlaw tradition. As I've already noted, first bananas like Bert Lahr and Bobby Clark rarely performed an erotic skit without the aid of a well-endowed showgirl as a nubile comic butt.

The great hidden subject of comedy, as Aristophanes was the first to demonstrate, is the conflict between Eros and Thanatos, or desire and death. This is why war was such anathema to this great comic playwright and why carnal relations remained his greatest hope for the perpetuation of human life.

(2010)

Alan Ayckbourn

Alan Ayckbourn is one of the most complete men of the theatre since Molière. Best known as a playwright, he has also functioned as a director, actor, stage manager, and sound designer, and let us not forget his tenure as artistic director of a major theatre in Scarborough. Not only does he discharge a large number of theatrical functions, he has also written an enormous number of plays for stage, radio, and children's theatre—over a hundred in fact—making him one of the most prolific dramatists since Lope de Vega (who wrote over eighteen hundred).

Ayckbourn continues that line of British farceurs that on stage has included Benn Levy and Ben Travers and Frederick Lonsdale and that later found its way into radio and TV in such entertainments as *The Goon Show* and *Monty Python's Flying Circus*. Ayckbourn himself is very conscious of the tradition in which he is writing. He numbers Oscar Wilde and Noel Coward among his influences and, if his adaptation of Richard Brinsley Sheridan's *A Trip to Scarborough* is any indication, can even see his way back to the great Irish farce masters of the eighteenth century, not only the precocious Richardson but the good-hearted Oliver Goldsmith as well.

Where his work departs from theirs, and seems more akin to such contemporary farces as Michael Frayn's *Noises Off*, is in the almost geometric nature of the plotting. His plays are nothing if not well-made. They would have impressed an architectural engineer. He writes works with two possible endings (*Intimate Exchanges*) and in three different time periods (*A Trip to Scarborough*). In *How the Other Half Loves*, he throws two different dinner parties on stage simultaneously, though they take place on two different evenings. In *The Norman Conquests*, he gives us three plays revolving around the same action, each occurring simultaneously in three different locations. And in *Bedroom Farce*, he brings on stage three separate bedrooms, all at the same time, where three (later four) actions are being performed before the audience simultaneously.

Perhaps the most intricate of these mechanisms is his more recent *House and Garden*. The evening is composed of two complete plays, both based on a stunt—namely that the same characters (and actors) appear in the two different actions, though performing in separate theatres. This results in a merry romp between the spaces by actors who have as much trouble catching their breath as remembering their lines. They are devoted to making certain that both plays take exactly two-and-one-half hours to perform. One can almost hear the metronome ticking.

This kind of theatrical approach has the potential to start a spectator ruminating about how to walk out of both plays simultaneously. As sometimes happens in Ayckbourn's more mechanical inventions, the gimmick is forced to do the work of the imagination. As for the content, Kenneth Tynan once wrote a piece called "The Lost Art of Bad Drama," in which he imagined a generic "Loamshire Play," where

> at no point may the plot or characters make more than a superficial contact with reality. Characters earning less than 1000 pounds a year should be restricted to small parts. . . . Women should declare themselves by running the palm of one hand up their victim's lapel and saying,"Let's face it, Arthur, you're not exactly indifferent to me."

He was describing, among many other West End creations, the plays of Alan Ayckbourn, which depend so heavily on the conventions of middle-class Suburbia. What he was failing to capture was this playwright's wit, humanity, and unfailing good nature. And also his capacity occasionally to have something loftier on his mind.

(2010)

Samuel Beckett

Although he died eleven years short of the year 2000, no writer better deserves the name of Millennium Poet Laureate than Samuel Beckett. A man obsessed with the old age of the world, Beckett endows his characters with diminished concentration, obscured intelligence, paralysis, paraplegia, memory loss, apatheia, and aphasia. They no longer seem to have procreative functions, only painful excretory ones.

This suggests how, for Beckett, existence was a brief, yet endless, purgatorial period stretching between our first mortal breath and our last—the verbal equivalent of Dali's limp watches sliding off a table or hanging on a tree. In *Endgame*, Clov defines yesterday as "that bloody awful day, long ago, before this bloody awful day." The passage of time in Beckett may be swift or tedious, but it is always "bloody awful."

Beckett's sense of time was deeply indebted to Chekhov's, an artist who also knew how slowly and quickly life can pass (*cf.* old Firs in *The Cherry Orchard*: "My life has slipped by as though I'd never lived.").

Never populated with more than five characters, his plays more often feature a solitary speaker, like the remorseful hermit of *Krapp's Last Tape* or the chattering housewife of *Happy Days* or the offstage female voice of *Rockaby* whispering off her aged parent in the rocker or, supremely, the disembodied mouth in *Not I*, crooning its lonely prosody in a void of Cimmerian gloom.

Perhaps his most oft-quoted lines are from *The Unnamable*: "I can't go on. I will go on." It is a sentiment he paraphrased often, most strikingly at the conclusion of *Waiting for Godot*:

"Well, shall we go?"
"Yes, let's go."
(*They do not move.*)

In his masterpiece *Godot*, Beckett dramatized the notion that life was a series of inconsequential and monotonous events by laying his first and second act side by side like two sets of railroad tracks. Recognizing that his art lent itself more readily to shorter statements, Beckett later economized his theme of a simultaneous today and tomorrow through a simple mechanical device in *Krapp's Last Tape*—a tape recorder. Of all Beckett's characters, Krapp seems the closest to his creator. His elegiac regret over an unfulfilled life is not unlike that of Jamie Tyrone in O'Neill's *A Long Day's Journey into Night* who says, quoting from Rossetti, "My name is Might-Have-Been. I am also called No More. Too Late. Farewell." Beckett is perhaps the quintessential playwright of existential rebellion, that futilitarian protest against a godforsaken naturalist universe that Shakespeare was the first to theatricalize in *King Lear*.

Nonetheless, however apocalyptic Samuel Beckett may have been about the old age of the world and the impotence of human beings, he continued to believe in the power of the written word and the immortality of works of art. For Samuel Beckett, life was damnation, but language was redemption. The human race can't go on. The human race will go on.

(2010)

Anton Chekhov

Anton Chekhov is arguably (for me, inarguably) the greatest playwright of the modern period. Yet, his reputation rests on a handful of plays—actually, only four have permanently entered the repertory. Each of these works, moreover, is written in an unmistakable signature style. Unlike, say, August Strindberg or Bertolt Brecht, Chekhov refrains from showy experimentation (except perhaps for Treplev's avant-garde shenanigans in *The Seagull*), and, unlike Henrik Ibsen, he is usually content with exploring a single social theme.

That theme is the radical change in Russian society that led to the revolutions of 1905 and 1917. About these changes, Chekhov takes no single political view. There are few playwrights who seem more aloof, more distant from the opinions of their characters, or who seem more deeply involved with what they do than what they say. Yet, despite this appearance of detachment, no other playwright seems as deeply invested in the future of the human race or more regretful about the prostration of the cultured elite before the forces of provincial darkness. Chekhov's writing is full of paradoxes—at the same time comic and tragic, engaged and impartial, subjective and objective. He creates no heroes or author's surrogates, yet we are never in doubt about the value he puts on human life.

Chekhov's four major plays sometimes seem to be one long play, focusing on the same class of aristocratic characters curdling in the country, engaged in the same debates about culture versus provincialism, and concluding with the same sense of ambiguous possibility, torn between hope and despair. *The Seagull* is unashamedly a play about literature and love, featuring two sets of actors (Madame Arkadina and Nina), two writers (Trigorin and Treplev), two views of the stage (realistic and visionary), and three love triangles (Treplev, Nina, and Trigorin; Arkadina, Trigorin and Nina; and Arkadina, Trigorin and Treplev). That the last of these has an incestuous component underlines the play's frequent parallels with Shakespeare's *Hamlet*.

Like *The Seagull*, *Uncle Vanya* is a play about hope and disillusionment. Vanya has lost all respect for his one-time idol, the academician Serebreyakov, and is in love with the professor's bored wife, Yelena. So too, in a more desultory way, is Doctor Astrov. But Yelena is too indolent to be unfaithful—though rarely in literature has a married man more deserved to be cuckolded. If the loss of belief in a professional ideal produces disillusionment, the loss of belief in the future produces despair. By the end of the play Vanya has come very close to the suicide that ended the life of Constantine Treplev.

Three Sisters, one of Chekhov's two indisputable masterpieces, is also about the loss of a comforting ideal. The Prozorov sisters have been spending most of their mature lives in a provincial military town, longing to return to Moscow. Masha is unhappily married to a schoolteacher, Irina is about to wed a soldier she admires but does not love, and Olga is stuck in a boring job. Meanwhile, their sister-in-law, Natasha (one of the most unredeemable characters Chekhov ever created), is eating away at their ancestral home like a carpenter ant, moving the sisters from one room to another and eventually out of the house in order to accommodate her crude maternal, social, and adulterous needs. *Three Sisters* is the bleakest play Chekhov ever wrote.

Composed with great difficulty while he was dying, *The Cherry Orchard* is, nevertheless, the most comical of Chekhov's full-length plays and may be his greatest work of art. In the tradition of a French mortgage melodrama but without heroes or villains, the play focuses on the loss of an ancestral estate whose aristocratic owners are too distracted to save it. In the speeches of the perpetual graduate student, Trofimov, we hear condemnations of the serf system and rumbles of the coming revolution, yet he, too, is so paralyzed he can do nothing about it but speechify. Ultimately the estate falls into the hands of the bourgeois Lopakhin, who, far from being a villainous overseer, is the hardest working man in the area.

Thus, without melodramatic or violent plotting, Chekhov sketches out a grand panorama of history through the lives of a few idle aristocrats. Like Lopakhin, the descendant of a serf, Chekhov leaves us in no doubt where his political sympathies lie. But as an artist who is humane to the marrow of his bones, he embraces virtually every one of his characters with deep-felt sympathy. Standing on the threshold of the modern world, Chekhov evokes a future in which, as Yeats prophesied, the best lack all ambition, and the worst are full of passionate intensity.

(2010)

Noel Coward

In many ways, Noel Coward is a unique British playwright. But he also belongs to a long tradition of English wit dramatists (many of them Anglo-Irish), who have been providing audiences with acerbic love tourneys ever since Beatrice first jousted with Benedict in *Much Ado About Nothing*. This tradition was to flower again after the Restoration under such seventeenth-century masters of the genre as John Dryden, George Etherege, William Wycherley, and, preeminently, William Congreve. It was to continue into the eighteenth century in the plays of Oliver Goldsmith and Richard Brinsley Sheridan. And it would experience another brilliant flowering in the nineteenth and twentieth centuries in the works of Oscar Wilde, Bernard Shaw, and Noel Coward.

More than that of any other country, the drama of Great Britain has been celebrated for its verbal dexterity. But what constitutes wit in one age can be something very different in another. Perhaps some clever graduate student will some day help us understand the seismic shift in style between the sensual, vitalist language of, say, Shakespeare's Sir John Falstaff in the Elizabethan period ("not only witty in myself, but the cause that wit is in other men") and the more effete wordplay of Etherege's Sir Foppington Flutter in the Restoration age. Whatever the case, it is not the corpulent Falstaff of *Henry IV* but the more elegant poseur of *The Man of Mode* who exercises the most lasting influence on future British dramatists, including Noel Coward.

Coward, by his own admission, was always a bit more of a lightweight than his witty predecessors. Nonetheless, he had a talent for brandishing the verbal saber and wielding the cutlass of repartee. Oscar Wilde said that the secret of art was treating trivial things humorously and humorous things trivially. Coward took that advice to heart. Still, unlike Wilde in his plays, Noel Coward did not always send off comic sparks. And while Wilde considered patriotism to be "the virtue of the vicious," Coward was not at all adverse to expressing jingoistic sentiments (for example, in the film *In Which We Serve* 1942). Nor did he shy away from romantic sentiments, as in the 1935 short play *Still Life* on which the 1945 film *Brief Encounter* was based. Despite his cutting wit, Coward was essentially a Romantic, and he continues to live not only in such sophisticated offerings as *Private Lives* (1930) and *Design for Living* (1933), but also in his repertory of sentimental songs like "I'll See You Again" and "Somewhere I'll Find You."

Coward was not just a playwright and composer; he was also a performer, and the character he developed—suave, soigné, elegant, and remote—was to become a crucial persona of English culture, almost defining for a while the nature of the English aristocracy. The Angry Young Men, among them John Osborne and Harold Pinter, thought they were rebelling against such "effete" bastions of the elite establishment as Coward and his ilk—and for a while Coward thought so, too. But the fact is that Osborne's dialogue, in *Look Back in Anger*, like Pinter's in *Betrayal*, would have been impossible without the witty banter of Noel Coward. He was, and continues to remain, the most powerful stylistic influence on modern British drama.

(2010)

Gilbert and Sullivan

Sir Arthur Sullivan's first successful comic opera, *Cox and Box* (1866), was written with another librettist, F. C. Burnand. But being about two long-lost brothers who prove to be inseparable twins, it might have been the story of Sullivan's lengthy, and sometimes stormy, collaboration with his librettist W. S. Gilbert. Sullivan always had ambitions to become a more serious musician (outside of his comic operas, he is best known as the composer of "Onward Christian Soldiers"), and Gilbert tried his hand from time to time with straight plays, usually featuring characters functioning under some supernatural influence. But the fourteen comic operas they wrote together over twenty-five years (1871–1896) have proved to be timeless masterpieces, products of a collaboration responsible for some of the most popular theatre pieces in the English language.

Gilbert and Sullivan sit very comfortably in a long-lived English tradition: the wit comedy that flourished on the English stage after the restoration of Charles II to the throne in 1660. (I have already mentioned this tradition in regard to

Noel Coward.) It cannot be sufficiently emphasized what a radical impact the Cromwellian Revolution had on English theatre. Having closed down London playhouses for eighteen years in 1642, the Puritans, who only let theatres open their doors for productions of opera. When the theatres reopened in 1660, English comedy had undergone a radical change. Where comic personae were once robust, red blooded, and muscular, they were now being characterized primarily by their delicate manners, their fashionable clothes, and, particularly, by their well-turned speech. Indeed, because of its powerful verbal emphasis, Restoration comedy has also been called "wit comedy," a form that extended into the eighteenth century when it produced a musical satire that might be considered a forerunner of Gilbert and Sullivan—John Gay's *The Beggar's Opera*.

Despite certain nods toward realism in the nineteenth-century plays of Tom Robertson, the prevalence of wit continued to inform the works of playwrights as diverse as Oscar Wilde, Bernard Shaw, Noel Coward, John Osborne, and Tom Stoppard. But with Gilbert and Sullivan, the tradition found its finest musical expression. Sullivan's calculated rhythms proved to be a perfect vehicle for Gilbert's often alliterative iambics ("I am the very model of a modern major-general"), while his passion for imagining long-lost children, rediscovered orphans, and miraculous transformations became the basis for plot twists and surprise turns that continue to delight audiences to this day.

Although Gilbert and Sullivan parodied Oscar Wilde in *Patience* (1881), surely Wilde was paying them the sincerest form of flattery in such plays as *The Importance of Being Earnest* (1895), when Jack Worthing, thinking he is feigning the name of Ernest in order to please his fiancée, actually turns out to be a long-lost child named Ernest, left in a handbag in a railroad station by his nurse, just as Buttercup had mistakenly exchanged

Ralph Rackstraw and the Captain in *HMS Pinafore* (1878). Bernard Shaw used similar absurd twists of fate to wind up the plots of his plays and so did a number of the English dramatists of the twentieth century, from Arthur Wing Pinero to Tom Stoppard.

The basic Gilbert and Sullivan technique, as Marc Shepherd shrewdly observes in an introduction written for *Gilbert and Sullivan in an Hour*, is a "preposterous idea followed logically to an absurd conclusion." A typical G & S plot, for example, depends on mistaken identity. Not only are Ralph Rackstraw and the *Pinafore's* Captain mixed up at birth, but so are the two young men in *The Gondoliers* (1889), the one a gondolier, the other the son of a king. The hero of *Yeomen of the Guard* (1888) is an imprisoned military captain, who disguises himself as a young lover. The Fairy Queen in *Iolanthe* (1882) reveals in the final act that she is the wife of the Lord Chancellor and presents him with a son he never knew he had. The pirates in *The Pirates of Penzance* (1879) all turn out to be noblemen who have gone wrong. And so forth.

All of this is performed through music of sometimes exquisite lyricism combined with looney lyrics by a master rhymester. Gilbert and Sullivan are clearly the very models of modern musical comedy, the ancestors of George and Ira Gershwin, Rodgers and Hart, Rodgers and Hammerstein, Lerner and Loewe, and Sondheim and Lapine, among others. Some think that, had he been born a few years later, W. S. Gilbert might very well have enrolled in the absurdist school of modern drama, being a more sanguine version of Eugene Ionesco. But Gilbert's real affinities are not only with English wits, but with the whimsical tradition of his near contemporary Lewis Carroll. Consider this quatrain from *The Pirates of Penzance*:

> I'm very well acquainted too
> with matters mathematical,

> I understand equations, both the
>   simple and quadratical,
> About binomial theorem I'm
>   teeming with a lot o' news –
> With many cheerful facts about
>   the square of the hypotenuse

It might work very well as a contribution to the Mad Hatter's tea party in *Alice's Adventures in Wonderland.*

(2010)

Lorraine Hansberry

Lorraine Hansberry was not the first female African-American playwright to be produced professionally in New York. That distinction belongs to Alice Childress and her 1949 off-Broadway production of *Florence*. But it was fewer than ten years later, in fact in 1959, that *A Raisin in the Sun* first appeared on Broadway to win the New York Theatre Critics Prize in a season that included plays by Eugene O'Neill and Tennessee Williams.

The fifties had already proved a significant decade for black writing. Indeed, it was during this time that James Baldwin published some of his strongest essays and novels (though his plays would be written later). But no one was prepared for such a powerful debut by a young African American woman who had not yet reached the age of twenty-nine. *A Raisin in the Sun* succeeded partly because it had the momentum of personal experience. Like Hansberry's character Walter Lee Younger, Jr., her father Carl was virtually obsessed with his right to live in any neighborhood he could afford; indeed, he pressed his case right up to the Supreme Court. But Hansberry's play was noteworthy not only as one of the first dramatizations of American blacks fighting desegregation but—as explored through the relationship of Joseph Asagai and Beneatha—it was one of the first to examine their relationship to African roots as well.

Despite her interest in socialism and communism, Hansberry was essentially a middle-class liberal with a deep concern for the rights of racial equality and sexual preference, as suggested by her marriage to a Jewish white man and by her later alleged lesbianism. Not all of her contemporaries responded warmly to her concerns. By this time, LeRoi Jones had transformed himself into Amiri Baraka and was taking a more revolutionary road than desegregation, while some avant-garde white playwrights were finding Hansberry's writing to be more familiar with the living room than the universe, being an extension of the domestic realism of Henrik Ibsen and Arthur Miller rather than the abstract worlds of Samuel Beckett and Eugene Ionesco.

Hansberry responded to these criticisms in her next play, produced in 1964, one year before she died. This was *The Sign in Sidney Brustein's Window*, which included some satire on a gay white avant-garde playwright, David Ragin (possibly based on Edward Albee). Neither this work, nor her posthumously produced *Les Blancs* (a response to Jean Genet's *Les Nègres* or *The Blacks*) succeeded on the New York stage, possibly because, unlike her first play, they were based more on personal positions than on lived experience. That such a small output has produced such a large reputation is a great tribute to her first play. But *A Raisin in the Sun*—by turns angry and compassionate, lyric and harsh, almost visionary in its drive toward equal rights—will always be remembered, both for its writing and for Lloyd Richards's initial production (featuring a riveting performance by Sidney Poitier as Walter Lee). Lorraine Hansberry died before reaching the age of thirty-five, but on the basis of this one play she continues to be an invaluable inspiration to such playwrights as Suzan-Lori Parks, Ntozake Shange, and Anna Deavere Smith, not to mention other black women dramatists of the present and the future.

(2010)

Henrik Ibsen

Some playwrights are celebrated for their power as builders, others for their power as breakers. Chekhov, preeminently, sometimes seems to be building one play over and over again, exploring the same provincial setting, and examining the same group of country characters. By contrast, the restless experimentation of Strindberg, that self-declared "world incendiary," is devoted to perpetual transformation of existing material. But it is very hard to catalogue Ibsen in either category; he is both architect and revolutionary, thus, builder *and* breaker. Often called the "father of modern drama," Ibsen created a radically new theatrical technique, in a series of explosive plays that, more than one hundred years after his death, continue to reverberate on our stages, tantalizing actors and directors as if they had been newly created.

True, Ibsen has been most widely known for the realistic contemporary dramas he developed out of the well-made plays of Scribe and Sardou during the 1870s and 1880s. Misinterpreted as "thesis" plays, works such *A Doll House*, *Ghosts*, and *The Wild Duck* persuaded audiences that Ibsen's primary theatrical purpose was essentially social and domestic and dedicated to exposing bad marriages and corrupt institutions.

Although Ibsen always maintained a fierce rebellion against the smug conventions of those he called the "pillars of society," he correctly maintained that "I have been more of a poet and less of a social philosopher than is commonly believed." The artist who first broke onto the world consciousness with such huge epic poems (mostly written in verse) as *Brand*, *Peer Gynt*, and *Emperor and Galilean* was hardly the comfortable burgher once described by H. L. Mencken as "a highly respected member of the middle class, well-barbered, ease-loving, and careful in mind . . . a safe and sane exponent of order, efficiency, honesty, and common sense . . . who believed in all the things that the normal, law-abiding citizen of Christendom believes in, from democracy to romantic love, and from the obligations of duty to the value of virtue." This about Ibsen, perhaps the most revolutionary dramatist who ever lived!

Ibsen's capacity to pursue a well-ordered domestic life while working to torpedo the Ark reminds us of Flaubert who once said you must be "regular and orderly in your life like a bourgeois so that you can be violent and original in your work." Ibsen, in exile from Norway for the first part of his life, certainly never neglected an opportunity to send shock waves through the community and, with his last semiautobiographical plays—*The Master Builder, John Gabriel Borkman, When We Dead Awaken*—he was even sending shock waves through his own soul. At the end, right before he suffered a massive stroke, he was speaking of his intention to enter the battlefield again "with new weapons and in new armor." Modern drama would not have been the same without him. The century that followed his death was shaped by his spirit, his courage, and his fiery vision.

(2010)

Tony Kushner

When Tony Kushner's monumental, two-part *Angels in America* opened in New York in 1993 (following performances at the Eureka Theatre, the Mark Taper, and the Royal Shakespeare Company), it was instantly clear that the American theatre had acquired another major playwright. As suggested by its subtitle—*A Gay Fantasia on National Themes*—*Angels* was a work that combined historical consciousness, artistic purpose, and gay pride. Indeed, in this play Kushner managed to suggest, at the same time, the epic ambitions of Eugene O'Neill, the sexual obsessions of Tennessee Williams, and the radical-liberal politics of Arthur Miller.

The play also exhibits a quality considerably less common among our native writers for the stage—sheer intellectual breadth. O'Neill's fascination with thinkers such as Nietzsche and Freud was rarely accompanied by any capacity to transform their ideas into penetrating drama. (Only in his later work, dedicated to more personal, nonintellectual themes, did O'Neill's intelligence begin to shine.) Williams, whose major influences were less philosophical than literary (August Strindberg, D. H. Lawrence, and Federico García Lorca), was always rather contemptuous of the rational intellect, preferring actions that were emotionally charged and unconsciously motivated. And Miller, while unquestionably a reflective man, never revealed any particular interest in abstract ideas, other than the Marxist coloration that tinged his rather conventional liberalism.

Kushner, on the other hand, is a highly educated thinker and omnivorous reader whose work is deeply informed by social, philosophical, and even theological ideas.

In part two of *Angels in America (Perestroika)*, for example, a doddering Bolshevik complains that humankind cannot function without the equivalent of Marxist theory. *Perestroika* provides that alternative by replacing Marxism with a totally sexualized theory of the universe.

A recent work—*The Intelligent Homosexual's Guide to Capitalism and Socialism with a Key to the Scriptures*—is inspired by George Bernard Shaw (who wrote the essay *The Intelligent Woman's Guide to Socialism and Capitalism*) and Mary Baker Eddy (who wrote *Science and Health With Key to the Scriptures*). Kushner is perhaps the first major American dramatist to demonstrate familiarity with the entire range of world thought and world drama, further demonstrated through his adaptations of works by Pierre Corneille, Heinrich von Kleist, Goethe, and Bertolt Brecht, not to mention Kushner's 1987 play *Hydriotaphia or The Death of Doctor Browne*, which was inspired by Sir Thomas Browne's reflections on urn burial and funerary customs.

On the other hand, Kushner is perfectly capable of creating works that are not driven by ideology or ideation, such as the musical he wrote with Jeanine Tesori, *Caroline or Change* (2002). This is a memory piece in couplets and quatrains about the transformations in race relations occurring in the South during Kushner's childhood in Louisiana. Like his other plays, the musical tells a political story through the agency of a personal anecdote, possibly autobiographical—here, a conflict between an angry black maid and a precocious eight-year-old Jewish boy. In his most imaginative stroke, Kushner turns the laundry room where Caroline, the maid, works into a fairy tale setting, in the manner of such children's stories as *The Little Engine That Could* and *Goodnight Moon*, anthropomorphizing such objects as a washing machine, a dryer, and a bus, for example, which are impersonated by an assortment of black singers.

In writing a play about race relations, Kushner was further revealing his engagement with many of the more controversial issues of our day. His play *Homebody/Kabul* (2001) was virtually a prediction of what was very soon to happen in the aftermath of 9/11.

And his criticism in the 2005 Steven Spielberg film, *Munich*, of Israel's treatment of Palestinian civilians after the terror attack in Germany got him in piping hot water with American Zionist groups (who later tried to block his honorary degree from Brandeis). In his willingness to criticize Israel, he stands in stark contrast to another major Jewish American dramatist, David Mamet, whose views on this and other political subjects are considerably to the right of Kushner's.

Perhaps even more controversial is Kushner's relentlessly homosexual interpretation of history as dramatized in *Angels in America*, where virtually every major character, including a lesbian angel, is gay. (The major exception, aside from the ghost of Ethel Rosenberg, is Joe Pitt's wife, and she is having a nervous breakdown.)

I do not mean to suggest that Kushner's political views are always partisan or sectarian. He is actually a warmhearted, sympathetic, and very complicated artist dedicated to helping audiences understand the bizarre time in which we live. No one I know has better dramatized the increasing sexual hypocrisy of right-wing America as embodied in the fifties by the character of Roy Cohen, dying of AIDS, yet refusing to admit he is gay—a foretaste of political hypocrisy today. As a character says in *Angels in America*, "In the new century, I think we will all be insane." Kushner dramatizes the spiritual instability of second-millennium America, creeping like a rotting vine through all our institutions, through all our waking lives and dreams.

(2010)

Arthur Miller

The name of Arthur Miller has always been synonymous with moral probity and social passion, even during the decades when his artistic reputation was in decline. Although almost half a decade has now passed since his death in 2005, one still feels vibrations from that resonant spirit. Miller's courage and conscience have made him an almost heroic figure in contemporary culture. But his artistic reputation seems to rest largely on four plays— *All My Sons*, *Death of a Salesman*, *A View From the Bridge*, and *The Crucible*—from among the approximately thirty-five that he wrote in his lifetime. (I personally would also have included his late, unpredictable *Ride Down Mount Morgan*.)

Miller was one of the last American playwrights to believe that his writing could change the world. (In this expectation, August Wilson was his legitimate heir.) It was a conviction tied to his debatable insistence that the soul of tragedy resided not in the lives of great people but in "the heart of the average man." In a sense, that was a liberal democratic political judgment. But he did not insist on this position throughout his career, partly as a result of historical chance. Miller was born between two great dramatic movements—the prewar era of political activism and the postwar era of existential absurdity. He reached artistic maturity toward the end of an age when most thinking people believed it essential to take strong stands against social and political injustice, either through engagement in activist art or through commitment to radical causes or both. But it was Miller's misfortune to have arrived on the scene just a few years too late to find true definition in the political struggles of the time.

Earlier radicals found ready-made solutions for social problems in Marx and Stalin. But Miller always seemed a little reticent about embracing a single ideology. As a result, as a political animal, he often gave the impression of having arrived at the parade after all the marching was over. He attended Communist meetings but never actually joined the Party. He was accepted into the Federal Theatre the very year that Congress put an end to it. And he was a little too young to get his seaman's papers on that pilot ship of theatre radicalism called The Group Theatre. This accident of timing helped him avoid some of the political missteps of activist drama and its often raw propagandistic disposition. It also left him without a coherent ideological framework with which to structure his political dissent. Attention must surely be paid! The passive voice reminds one of the classic political evasions: "Mistakes were made." Yes, but by whom?

Coming of age in the forties, Miller was nonetheless a premature child of the thirties, deeply influenced by such passionate pioneers as Hallie Flanagan Davis, leader of The

Federal Theatre, and by the style of the Group playwrights, most notably Clifford Odets. But perhaps the greatest stylistic influence on his work was that of another celebrated Group member, Elia Kazan, who became Miller's chief director and collaborator until their well-publicized split over the issue of naming names to the House Un-American Activities Committee. If Miller's work appeared to lose some of its vigor after that falling out, part of the reason lies in the loss of Kazan's influence, though the two men were briefly reunited during the Lincoln Center production of Miller's *After the Fall*.

In that play, as in his autobiographical memoir, *Timebends*, Miller very honestly examined his ambivalent attitude toward celebrity—mainly personified by his short-lived marriage to Marilyn Monroe. And in a way, the final years of his career were an effort to expiate that momentary fall from grace. His passionate concern for human freedom, ecology, and justice as president of PEN International was a return to his early sense that literature could function as an instrument of change. Great, good, bad, or indifferent, Arthur Miller's work has always borne the stamp of a great conscience, always paying witness to what was worth criticizing in the American character and what was worth celebrating.

(2010)

Eugene O'Neill

Eugene O'Neill is unequivocally the greatest dramatist America ever produced. Yet, his reputation will very probably rest on his last plays, a few of them produced only after his death. A restless experimenter who singlehandedly yanked a provincial culture onto the world stage through his passion for European drama, O'Neill followed a career arc very similar to that of his idol, August Strindberg. Exploring masks, doppelgangers, soliloquies, and dream plays, he finally settled into a realistic style more akin to that of Henrik Ibsen, focusing on what he called "the family Kodak" of his own benighted life.

O'Neill's earlier plays are hardly without value. Indeed, they earned him numerous Pulitzers and, in 1936, the Nobel Prize. Some, like *Desire Under the Elms*, contain powerful scenes; some, like *The Great God Brown*, have interesting themes; and some, like those long endurance trips, *Mourning Becomes Electra* and *Strange Interlude*, are sustained by the sheer force of the author's will. Still, the bulk of O'Neill's writings before his one comedy, *Ah, Wilderness!*, in 1933 are like the groping preparatory sketches of one who had to write badly in order to write well. No major dramatist, with the possible exception of Shaw, has produced so many second-rate plays.

Ah, but with *The Iceman Cometh* and *A Long Day's Journey Into Night*—and to a lesser extent with *Hughie* and *A Moon for the Misbegotten*—O'Neill developed from a self-conscious stammering experimenter into an eloquent artist, concentrating a fierce bullish power into fables of reality and illusion, shot through with flashes of humor, but pervaded by a sense of melancholy over the condition of being human. The hiatus between *Ah, Wilderness!* and *Days Without End*, both written in 1933, and his work on *The Iceman Cometh*, written in 1939 but not produced until 1946, was the longest of his career. But the time lapse demonstrated that something more portentous was happening in O'Neill's life than the annual production of new, and often imperfect, works written in imitation of some European playwriting idol.

The fact is he was beginning to write about his family, uncovering painful secrets that hitherto had been shrouded in darkness. Instead of feeling superior to his subjects, he was taking his own condition as a metaphor for the cankered nature of the land. With these honest, remorseless probes into his own past, O'Neill began to approach the conditions of truth in his plotting and poetry in his writing as he elected to look the Gorgon full in the face.

In power and insight, O'Neill still remains unsurpassed among American dramatists, and, indeed, it is doubtful if there would have been an American drama without him. But it is for his last plays, I believe, that he will be remembered—those extraordinary gall stones that he surgically excised from himself in pain and suffering, a sick and tired man in a shuttered room, unable to bear much light.

(2010)

Luigi Pirandello

Pirandello rarely wrote autobiographical plays. Yet, he is one of the most subjective dramatists of the modern period, and certainly the most self-conscious. He is always present as a hovering reflective intelligence—commenting, expostulating, and conceptualizing. That is why Pirandello describes himself as a "philosophical writer." He soaks his plots and characters in a particular sense of life.

As a result, Pirandello has often been accused of being cerebral, which he does not deny. "One of the novelties I have given modern drama," he writes, "consists in converting the intellect into passion." After Ibsen and Shaw, this is hardly a novelty, but Pirandello is certainly the first to convert abstract thought into passion—to formulate a theoretical philosophy in theatrical terms.

People tend to think of Pirandello as an experimental dramatist, but only his great theatre trilogy (*Six Characters in Search of an Author, Tonight We Improvise, Each in His Own Way*) can be truthfully called formal breakthroughs. The rest of his forty-five plays, adventurous as they are in theme, are relatively conventional in form. The basic Pirandellian conflict is internal—between the mask one shows to the world and the actual face of the suffering individual. In *Right*

You Are (If You Think You Are), Pirandello makes his recurrent point that the truth of one's character must remain forever concealed if one is to survive in an intrusive society.

This is what Pirandello means by *construire*, building oneself up. Humans make themselves into constructions, taking on various roles (father, priest, neurotic) for the sake of personal protection. This protective coloring makes the typical Pirandellian hero a kind of actor, a character in disguise. This is certainly the situation in Pirandello's masterpiece, *Enrico IV*, where the hero—under the delusion for years that he is a Holy Roman Emperor—elects to maintain that mad role when he finally recovers his sanity.

It is Pirandello's attraction to role-playing that makes his theatre trilogy the most powerful and original of his plays. In *Six Characters*, there is conflict between the written characters, who can never deviate from the two scenes the author wrote for them, and the actors who are asked to bring these scenes to life. The characters long to have their interrupted lives completed, yet the actors parody and vulgarize their reality to a ludicrous degree.

Pirandello's influence on the drama of our time has been incalculable. He is the ultimate embodiment of that modern genre that Lionel Abel called "metatheatre," where the play is intended as more than a finite object and the action continues after the curtain comes down. (In *Tonight We Improvise*, the fourth wall is broken and the audience becomes a character in the play.) It is entirely possible that Pirandello will be remembered more as a great theoretician than as a great practitioner. But while the playwrights who follow Pirandello may be better artists, none would have been the same without him. And he has left us some extraordinary plays wherein his melancholy view of human existence still sounds its elegiac music.

(2010)

Theresa Rebeck

Sigmund Freud once got himself in a lot of hot water by asking "What do women want?" An equally inflammatory question today might be, "What do women playwrights want?" The obvious answer is that women playwrights want the same things as male playwrights—access to production, percentage of the gross, audience admiration, critical endorsement, coveted prizes, and inscriptions on the walls of fame. After so many years of pressing their faces against the sweetshop window, they desire and deserve all the chocolates and caramels on display.

Theresa Rebeck has been working hard and productively over recent years to merit her place at the candy counter. Judging by her prodigious creative output, she is a continuously evolving artist. Judging by the quality of her plays, she is a truly independent spirit. Granted, she can occasionally lapse into defensive outbursts, especially when provoked by some insensitive critic or dimwitted dinner partner. But the best of Rebeck's theatrical writing, like that of all good writers, has always been gender neutral. From Lillian Hellman (who made Regina Hubbard in *The Little Foxes* even more ruthless than her male counterparts) to Paula Vogel (who short-circuited the prevailing assumptions about child abuse in *How I Learned to Drive* and about pornography in *Hot 'n Throbbin'*) to Suzan-Lori Parks (who resented being told her "plays are about what it's about to be black—as if that's all we think about. My life is not about race. It's about being alive.") to Wendy Wasserstein (who satirized gender studies and political correctness in *Third*), not to mention dozens of other gifted woman writers, the best of them, whether embracing feminist politics or not, have usually managed to avoid ideological clichés.

Rebeck is just as sophisticated about these issues as any woman writing. She has not only composed many plays, she has also employed many forms, including television and the novel, and mastered the art of dynamic human relationships. The play she collaborated on with Alexandra Gersten-Vassilaros, called *Omnium Gatherum* (2003), holds a high place as the *locus classicus* of dramatic works about 9/11, featuring one of the most goofy radical chic dinner parties since Shaw's *Heartbreak House*. Her recent play *Mauritius* (2007) is less about collecting injustices than about stamp collecting. *Spike Heels* (2006) is a poisonously funny sex triangle featuring hilariously abusive dialogue.

Although a declared feminist, Rebeck almost never falls into stereotypes as a writer, though she has been quoted (in the introduction to her plays) as saying that "gender bias is the hidden sin of the American theatre." Isn't it time that that academic jargon—"gender"—was retired from the modern lexicon? ("What did you do with your boyfriend last night?" "We had gender together.") More important is the fact that Rebeck's playwriting is almost entirely free of such reductionism. Her true subject, as she correctly says, is not gender issues but what it means to be an American: "the way David Hare examines what it means to be British or Brian Friel examines what it means to be Irish." Rebeck knows that she cannot ignore the social issues of the day, but she recognizes, like Chekhov, that it is not her job to solve problems, only to present them correctly.

This is something she has done with genuine gusto in her adaptation of Aeschylus's *Agamemnon*, *The Water's Edge* (2006), and even better in her electrifying comedy, *The Scene* (2006). In the latter play, Rebeck demonstrates how effectively she can transcend extra-dramatic chatter and get on with writing a lively account of the aesthetic and moral failures of show folk. Actually, the play is not unlike David Rabe's *Hurly Burly*, a similar probe into entertainment culture with the same raucous and remorseless exposure of human folly.

I have full confidence that Rebeck will continue to pour her creative juices into artistry rather than activism. She has enough smarts, enough energy, enough fearlessness—and enough "fuck you"—to take a place among her most gifted contemporaries—and thus be assured of a permanent place in the sweet shop of American dramatic literature.

(2010)

Sarah Ruhl

Still barely thirty-five, Sarah Ruhl has swiftly become one of the most frequently produced dramatists of our time. Not too long ago, when one would have been required to add the qualifier "female" dramatists; this would have been unimaginable. But there has been a large accumulation of plays by women in the last few decades, making sexual identification less important. Still, though progress has been made, women still experience prejudice in the theatre world. For instance, the plays of female writers continue to be less produced than those of male writers.

Older people like myself, with longer memories than Ruhl's typical audience, remember a time when women playwrights were as scarce as male secretaries. After naming Susan Glaspell, one of Eugene O'Neill's contemporaries at the Provincetown Playhouse in the teens of the last century, and Sophie Treadwell (author of *Machinal*) in the twenties and, most notably, Lillian Hellman, in the thirties, forties, fifties, and sixties, the number of significant women in the profession would have been exhausted. That all began to change with the advent of feminism in the sixties. Still, glass ceilings continue to block entry into some American professions, including, to some extent, the theatre. But the presence of maturing female playwrights like Sarah Ruhl will hopefully shatter those ceilings. Indeed, one might ask if there would be American drama today without Maria Irene Fornes,

Lorraine Hansberry, Adrienne Kennedy, Paula Vogel, Beth Henley, Wendy Wasserstein, Marsha Norman, Suzan-Lori Parks, Tina Howe, Caryl Churchill, Lynn Nottage, Anna Deavere Smith, Rebecca Gilman, Theresa Rebeck, in addition to all those I have neglected to mention.

One of Paula Vogel's students in her celebrated playwriting program at Brown (Vogel now heads the department at the Yale School of Drama), Sarah Ruhl has quickly become a mainstay of the resident theatre movement, as well as off-Broadway. She first became known to New York audiences with her comedy about immigrant women and middle-class wives, *The Clean House* (2004), the earliest of the plays she has recently been producing at a remarkable rate—about one every year. Other productions include plays based on Greek mythological themes such as *Eurydice* (2003) and *Demeter in the City* (2006), as well as plays inspired by other writers and forms, like *Orlando* (1998) and *Passion Play, A Cycle* (2005).

She attracted critical interest most recently with *In the Next Room, or the Vibrator Play* (2009), a work that represents a considerable advance. While some works like *The Clean House* are sometimes driven by a sitcom premise (a Brazilian woman who hates cleaning houses and allows the heroine's sister to do it, surreptitiously) and others like *Dead Man's Cell Phone* (2007) occasionally descend into excessive cuteness, *In the Next Room* shows real maturity in technique and subject matter. Set in the late nineteenth century against the background of the invention of electricity, it is a study of the relationship between science and sensuality, or decorum and passion, as demonstrated through the attempt by the heroine's doctor-husband to cure hysteria by inducing orgasm. Intersexual and interracial like most of Ruhl's writing, the play employs a semidetached, purposely naïve, and vaguely surreal style to make important points about race, marriage, and sexual relations.

Ruhl is not afraid of taking on big subjects, and, young as she is, she still has the time to cover a lot of ground. She is a playwright to be watched—bold, fearless, and intrepid.

(2010)

Arthur Schnitzler

Arthur Schnitzler is the most precarious of playwrights, suspended as he is between the confident assurance of European classicism and the skeptical vertigo of Modernism. At times, his plays display the conventions of French farce or nineteenth-century melodrama in the style of his Hungarian contemporary, Ferenc Molnár. At the next moment, they plunge us into the dizzying whirlpools of Luigi Pirandello or the sexual tidal waves of Frank Wedekind.

As Carl Mueller suggests in a fascinating reflection on the playwright, part of Schnitzler's elusiveness can be attributed to the fact that he was born a Jew during a particularly anti-Semitic period in European history. Coming upon the scene a few years after Austria, having lost its hegemony, united with Hungary, he died just a few months after Hitler came to power in Germany. This period, as Amos Elon tells us in his illuminating book, *The Pity of It All*, was perhaps one of the most trying times in history for Germanic Jewry, which had hitherto enjoyed relative tolerance and respect. And it helped shape his ethnic consciousness when other Jews—Felix Mendelssohn and Heinrich Heine for example—were ignoring their heritage and becoming Lutherans.

Like Sigmund Freud, Schnitzler was a physician who specialized in psychiatry, the insights of which play a large role in his work. And like that other medical man of the theatre, Anton Chekhov, he was fascinated with class differences and diagnosed human behavior as being shaped by similar motivations. But perhaps the dramatist with whom Schnitzler shared the most common ground was August Strindberg, particularly in their common emphasis on human sexuality and their mutual belief that it was in the nature of humankind (or rather womankind in the case of Strindberg) to be sexually unfaithful.

Both in *Reigen* (*Round Dance*) and his *Anatol* plays, for example, Schnitzler focuses exclusively on sexual infidelity. *Reigen* is virtually a merry-go-round of promiscuity since each of its ten scenes begins and ends with a switch of sexual partners, just as each of the seven *Anatol* one-acts concludes with an instance of sexual intercourse. It was partly because of this erotic emphasis that Schnitzler's plays were so often banned or censored or labeled as "Jewish filth," even though by today's standards they seem relatively tame. (The lights usually dim before any sexual act is consummated.)

Schnitzler's influence on contemporary theatre has been subtle but persistent. Although his plays are seldom produced, they are often adapted. For example, in 1991 Larry Gelbart converted *Reigen* into a satiric political comedy called *Power Failure*, while Stanley Kubrick used Schnitzler's novel *Traumnovelle* as the basis for his last movie, filmed in 1999, called *Eyes Wide Shut*. (I suspect Adrian Lyne's 2002 movie *Unfaithful* with Diane Lane also owes a debt to a Schnitzler work, *Liebelei*.) Arthur Schnitzler remains one of our most under-appreciated playwrights despite incisions into the human heart that remain sharp and penetrating.

(2010)

William Shakespeare

Despite William Shakespeare's epic status in the theatrical canon, one gnawing issue still plagues his legacy: the authorship controversy, or the assumption that Shakespeare did not write his own plays.

Indeed, virtually every literary Shakespearean contemporary—the Earl of Oxford, the Earl of Derby, Sir Francis Bacon,

Christopher Marlowe, Mr. W. H., even Queen Elizabeth herself—has been proposed as the true author. And not all of the conspiracy theorists were loonies; even Sigmund Freud declared himself an Oxfordian.

The reason? Unlike Marlowe and Jonson, Shakespeare never went to university. He only attended Stratford grammar schools.

Well, apart from the fact that Stratford grammar schools provided a classical education more rigorous than that provided by most contemporary American universities (the majority of which, by the way, no longer even require a Shakespeare course in their English Departments), it is absurd to argue that you need a higher degree in order to invent Shakespeare's verses, plots, and characters. This I attribute to modern academic snobbery, where imagination is often confused with scholarship.

Did Mozart have a college education? Did Molière? Did Michelangelo? Actually, the greatest artists of history have often been instinctual, self-taught geniuses who managed their research without the aid of tutors or textbooks.

The most convincing proof that Shakespeare wrote his own plays is the fact that Ben Jonson said he did. Jonson, who had a very strong classical education, was one of the most envious men in literature. He would, therefore, have been the first to declare Shakespeare an impostor had that been so. Instead, in the funeral eulogy appended to the First Folio, Jonson declared that Shakespeare, whom he loved "this side of idolatry," was "a monument without a tomb," a tribute he offered despite the fact that Shakespeare had "little Latin and less Greek," much less a piece of academic foolscap.

The next controversial thing about Shakespeare is his identity as a person. It is very hard to draw his personality from his plays, probably because he likely had none, or very little, other than the geniality that everybody attributed to him. Characters poured through him, and possessed him, like ghosts around a séance table. But, to be responsive to such visitations, an artist is often forced to drain himself of personal characteristics and become an empty vessel. We know that Shakespeare rarely, if ever, invented his plots. Instead, he took a borrowed story and poured characters into it, speaking the most powerful and beautiful language ever uttered. If you look at the original models for Hamlet, Falstaff, Iago, and Lear, indeed all of Shakespeare's major characters, they all seem rather puny. What Shakespeare gives them is the heft, arc, and pitch of genius.

We concentrate so much on Shakespeare's language and characters that we sometimes fail to appreciate his philosophy. Inheriting all the prejudices of his time—misogyny, machismo, anti-semitism, racism, and that early version of Intelligent Design known as the Elizabethan World Picture—he eventually managed to abandon most of them and envision a universe as malignant as the one we inhabit today. It is the misanthropic universe of Timon and Lear where ingratitude and self-interest reign. It is the savage nature goddess of Iago and Edmund, red in tooth and claw. And although it exists in parallel with the humanistic world of Rosalind and Desdemona and Prospero, it is also a predatory environment, where "humanity must perforce prey upon each other, like monsters of the deep." For his understanding of all those contradictory things, and for being the kind of instinctual genius that exalts the human race, Shakespeare will always be, in Jonson's words, "not of an age, but for all time."

(2010)

George Bernard Shaw

George Bernard Shaw in a five-minute essay? It usually takes at least an hour for him to clear his throat. Shaw is a writer who doesn't simply compose a play; he builds an entire social, political, religious, and philosophical scaffold around it. Scorning the role of "mere" artist in favor of his preferred function of "artist-philosopher," Shaw invariably offers discourses not just on the subject of the play, but on the conduct of humanity, the state of society, and the nature of the universe. Ann Whitefield's concluding line in Man and Superman, "Go on talking, Jack," is clearly Shaw's self-mocking recognition of his own incorrigible loquacity.

Can such an inveterate rhetorician be listed among the great dramatic artists? Was Shaw a poet or—like Eugene O'Neill—a man who simply had the makings of one? That question continues to be debated in spite of the fact that few of his illustrious Irish contemporaries—neither Joyce, nor Wilde, nor Yeats—held Shaw in more than mild esteem. (Indeed, Yeats dismissed him as "the chosen author of very clever journalists.") Still, at least one major artist, T. S. Eliot, recognized there was a poet in Bernard Shaw, that is, "until he was born—and the poet in Shaw was stillborn."

What Eliot was suggesting, I think, is that Shaw's poetic nature was often crippled by his intrusive intellect and, even more, by his odd incapacity to see the darker corners of human nature. (That role he gave to the Devil in Man and Superman.) Shaw's blindness to evil may explain why he was still praising Hitler and Mussolini long after those dictators began pursuing less salubrious goals than making the trains run on time. Shaw rejected Darwin for similar reasons, because he simply could not contemplate an arbitrary and indifferent system that "banished mind from the universe." In place of Darwin's evolutionary theories he substituted Lamarck's crackpot ideas about Creative Evolution, a concept that seems to have had as much basis in fact as Intelligent Design, which it resembles. And although he was among the first to recognize the importance of Henrik Ibsen, Shaw's early study, The Quintessence of Ibsenism, transformed that radical anarchist into a species of domesticated social worker, not unlike Shaw's own Andrew Undershaft building comfortable Levittowns for homeless employees.

On the other hand, it is undeniable that Shaw wrote some really sublime plays, the best in my opinion being *Heartbreak House*. His most tragic and pessimistic work, *Heartbreak House* found its genesis in Shaw's despair over World War I (though the author delayed its opening until the war was over). It was a play in which Shaw, for a moment, stopped grinning in order to perform a CAT scan on the worsening human condition. The result was an apocalyptic fantasy that not only faulted human institutions but the nature of humankind itself with an eloquence that went much deeper than reason. In *Heartbreak House*, the poet in Shaw is no longer stillborn; he is completely functional and working at full strength.

Shaw also wrote a number of sublime social comedies with philosophical overtones, among them *Pygmalion*, *Misalliance*, *Man and Superman*, and *Major Barbara*. These and other of his comedies are genuine contributions to dramatic literature. But while we value Shaw's ruminations on the life force, creative evolution, the superman, phonetics, eugenics, and other passing concerns, we value even more the intelligence, eloquence, and intensity with which they have been expressed. For the issues themselves have begun to disappear into the misty land of bright ideas. Will Shaw's plays begin to fade as well, or will they survive, despite their obsolescent view of humankind, as penetrating works of art? There is no question they will always find validity as lively artifacts of Victorian comedy. The final judgment on Shaw has yet to be made. But for the moment, he still holds our attention with his wonderful surface brilliance, even as his pre-Holocaust optimism is being contradicted by exploding bombs and tribal slaughter.

(2010)

Sam Shepard

Sam Shepard's unpredictable career falls into at least two periods, possibly three. The first features the East Village space cadet of *La Turista* (1967), *The Unseen Hand* (1969), and *Cowboy Mouth* (1971), when Shepard seems to be dreaming poetic phantasmagorias through a haze of narcotics. At this time, Shepard, a companion to his collaborator on *Cowboy Mouth*, Patti Smith, and a drummer for The Holy Modal Rounders, is bouncing his plays against an aural background of hard rock music, alternating with the nasalized oral twang of Northern California. Perhaps the best known play of this period, *The Tooth of Crime* (1971), actually features a combat between an older and a younger musician for primacy in the world of rock.

Hallucination, frenzied music, and the battle between age and youth—these are the hallmarks of generally short plays that brought their author a growing reputation and a limited off-off-Broadway audience. During a trip to London in the early 1970s, however, when Shepard was exposed to the explosive eloquence of the Royal Court Theatre movement and met such masters of the form as Harold Pinter, his art underwent a significant sea change. This led to what he once described to me as his "English period," where the typical Shepard dreamscape is forced into the background, lurking behind an essentially realistic and domestic *mise en scène*.

One of the earliest plays in this genre is *Curse of the Starving Class* (1978), its title a mischievous gloss on the old adage that "drink was the curse of the working class." Set in a run-down kitchen, complete with refrigerator and stove, the play seemed to suggest that Shepard was abandoning his expressionist legacy and joining Miller, Williams, and Albee in the world of American family drama. So did another play of that period, *Buried Child* (1978), which, located in the Midwest rather than California, is an almost Ibsenite allegory about how the hidden sins of a family are eventually exposed to view, like vegetables pushing through the fallow earth. The final image of Tilden coming on stage with a dead baby in his arms encased in husks of corn is one of the most powerful in all modern drama.

It was during this "English period" that Shepard found fame as a Hollywood actor and was nominated for an Academy Award for his performance as Chuck Yeager in *The Right Stuff*. Having repaired a broken front tooth, married a beautiful and gifted movie star (Jessica Lange), and built a stable of horses, Shepard seemed to be falling victim to the curse of the celebrity class. He even began to play polo, like Tom Buchanan in Fitzgerald's *The Great Gatsby*, and constructed a swimming pool, like Gatsby himself. (Also like Gatsby, he probably never used it.) But Shepard was hardly trying to live out his Platonic image of himself. Quite the contrary, it was toward the end of this period that Shepard began his most serious and dangerous work, first as a critic of the Protestant ethic—as well as of family and marital relationships—in such plays as *True West* (1980) and *A Fool for Love* (1983) and then as a critic of America's growing belligerent posture in the world and its unchecked ability to suspend civil rights.

Perhaps because of his occasional collaborations with Joseph Chaikin of the activist Open Theatre, Shepard was beginning to display a new, or perhaps newly reinforced, political conscience in such plays as *States of Shock* (1991), *Simpatico* (1993), and *The God of Hell* (2004). In that last work particularly, Shepard offers what may very well be the fiercest and most radical critique to date of the government rationale for the Iraq War, American torture procedures, and invasions of privacy. Thus, Shepard has exchanged a radical formal trademark for a radical social-political agenda, following the same path as Henrik Ibsen who suppressed the powerful poetic instincts he displayed in such earlier plays as

Brand and *Peer Gynt* in order to document the sins of modern life in such plays as *Ghosts* and *The Wild Duck*. In Ibsen's case, this was the act of a genuine saint of the theatre. In the case of Sam Shepard, it is the choice of an artist who never ceases to grow, to explore, to confront, and to listen to new music.

(2010)

Sophocles

Sophocles, whose dates are 497-406 BC, was only twenty years younger than Aeschylus, but he seems to have inhabited an entirely different world. "My dramatic wild oats were imitations of Aeschylus's pomp," Plutarch quotes him as saying, "then I evolved my own harsh mannerisms. And finally I embraced that style which is best, as most adapted to the portrayal of human nature." The art scholar Margarete Bieber suggests we keep a certain statue of Sophocles in mind when trying to understand the Greek conception of the hero—a grave beauty of countenance and bearing, expressing physical strength and an ordered soul.

We should also keep his plays in mind, since they are among the most perfect and profound works of drama ever written. During his long and reputedly untroubled life, Sophocles wrote over one hundred tragedies, of which only a precious seven survive, mostly from his middle and late periods. His abiding theme is human nature in relation to the universe, and his quintessential tragic hero is the man with a double nature, both blessed and cursed.

Typical of these is *Philoctetes* whose hero, a wounded warrior of the Trojan War, has been isolated on an island because of his foul-smelling wound, but who possesses a magic bow necessary for the victory of the Greeks. (In *The Wound and the Bow*, Edmund Wilson made Philoctetes into the symbol of the modern artist, supremely gifted, yet odorous and offensive.) The same is true of Oedipus, especially in *Oedipus at*

Colonus, where he is a blind old man, banished by humans and cursed by the gods, yet still capable of bestowing blessings on Athens before he dies.

On the surface, *Oedipus*, *Oedipus at Colonus*, and *Antigone* would seem to constitute a trilogy since they all tell stories of the same family in relatively consecutive fashion. But these three plays were written at separate stages in the playwright's career, and they are not always factually or chronologically consistent. In *Oedipus*, for example, written in 426 BC, Oedipus banishes himself from Thebes. In *Oedipus at Colonus*, written twenty-one years later, a year before the playwright's death, Oedipus claims he was banished by Creon. Similarly, *Antigone*, though historically the last play in the Oedipus cycle, was actually written first. Most important is the way that Sophocles humanizes Attic tragedy. While clearly a religious man, Sophocles dramatically reduces the role of the Olympians in his plays. The gods rarely appear on stage; the *deus ex machina* stays in the wings, collecting dust. That is why the role of prophecies and oracles, the human instruments of the gods, grows exponentially more important.

Sophocles remains supreme in his capacity to dramatize angry, argumentative encounters—between, say, Antigone and Creon, or between Oedipus and Tiresias. But the thing for which Sophocles is best remembered is the perfection of the tragic art, which is why he was so clearly Aristotle's favorite playwright and the model for neoclassicists ever after. In *Oedipus*, Sophocles created what may very well be the most perfectly plotted play ever composed. And while Aeschylus was often inchoate and obscure, Sophocles always remains clear and melodious, writing dramatic verse that almost hums, which earned him from his contemporaries the nickname of "The Bee."

(2010)

Tom Stoppard

Yeats once said that writers who argue with themselves create poetry while those who argue with others create rhetoric. Tom Stoppard represents a third development—a writer who argues with the arguers and creates commentary. After the socially engaged, angry young playwrights of the fifties, Stoppard led the next postmodern stage of British drama. By adding both an epigrammatic style and scholarly approach to theatre, he moved it backward in form and forward in subject matter.

One can only speculate about the reasons for these contradictory literary directions. Some have surmised that Tom Stoppard, born Tom Straussler in Czechoslovakia and raised the stepson of a British army major, had an identity crisis when he learned later in life that his parents were Jewish. Others have suggested that Stoppard's fondness for academicism— he often resembles an Elizabethan "university wit"—is a common quality of autodidacts. (Stoppard never attended a university.) Whatever the case, from the moment Stoppard burst upon the English stage with his play about two footnote characters in *Hamlet* called *Rosencrantz and Guildenstern Are Dead* (1966), indebted to *Waiting for Godot*, he was essentially writing dissertations about existing academic, scientific, literary, and political icons.

If this made a few of his spectators feel like retired learners taking refresher courses at an adult extension school, it also had the advantage of introducing audiences to arcane subjects of considerable interest. In the last three decades, for example, Stoppard has reflected on A. J. Ayer and logical positivism (*Jumpers*, 1972); on Tristan Tzara, Vladimir Lenin, James Joyce, and literary-political exile (*Travesties*, 1974); on Byron, Hobbes, Newton, Fermat, and hydroponic gardening (*Arcadia*, 1993); and on A. E. Houseman, Walter Pater, Benjamin Jowett, Oscar Wilde, and male love (*The Invention of Love*, 1997). In a more recent offering, the epic nine-hour trilogy called *The Coast of Utopia* (2002), Stoppard covers the entire history of Russian Idealism, as represented by six major figures of the prerevolutionary intelligentsia. Eric Bentley once wrote a book called *The Playwright as Thinker*. How would he categorize Tom Stoppard, I wonder? The playwright as research professor?

Stoppard researches his subjects with considerable learning and wit, not to mention exemplary literary skill. What critics have found missing is the pulse and heartbeat of genuine feeling—though this is less of a problem in his best works: a play like *The Real Thing* (1982) and a movie like *Shakespeare in Love* (1998). Aristotle believed that the highest purpose of tragedy was to inspire in the spectator pity and terror for a character's fate. Stoppard's work more often produces awe and admiration for the playwright's wit. This was also the achievement of such inspired comic writers as Oscar Wilde and Noel Coward, and sometimes Bernard Shaw, whose rhetorical tradition Stoppard appears to be tapping. Stoppard's originality consists in combining witty exercises with self-conscious intellectual commentary, and that would seem to be his chief contribution to postmodern drama.

(2010)

Frank Wedekind

It is an irony of literature that one of the wildest and most erotic of German dramatists should have been named after one of America's most mild-mannered moralists, the Philadelphian diplomat whom D. H. Lawrence liked to deride as "snuff-colored Ben Franklin."

Benjamin Franklin Wedekind was anything but "snuff-colored." He shared with D. H. Lawrence a compulsion to probe the dark corners of the human libido, the secret currents flowing under the rational surface of bourgeois life.

Freud, Krafft-Ebbing, and others were also writing about sex in this straitlaced time, in a Germany that was arguably the most repressed state in Europe. Although Wedekind shared with these scientists a conviction that constrained libidos could lead to tragic consequences, Wedekind's purposes were hardly theoretical or therapeutic. He was to sexual provocation what Bakunin was to political provocation: an extremist on behalf of absolute freedom, which sometimes made him, like Bakunin, look like a social outlaw.

Wedekind's two Lulu plays (*Earth Spirit* and *Pandora's Box*) are the best examples of his moral anarchy, which is why they still have the power to alienate audiences. (Lee Breuer's production of this duo in the second season of the American Repertory Theatre lost us half our subscribers!) Lulu is a totally amoral courtesan who follows her desires regardless of moral, spiritual, or canon law. In her mind, sex is a form of power as well as pleasure, which is why Wedekind's idea of poetic justice at the end of *Pandora's Box* is to have Lulu in London murdered by Jack the Ripper, who thereupon cuts out her vulva, washes his hands in a bucket, and leaves the stage, muttering "I'm so lucky. I'm so lucky."

Wedekind's other erotic masterpiece is *Spring Awakening*, a play about the tragic flowering of adolescent sexual desire in a time without sexual enlightenment. A number of young people in this play suffer either death or imprisonment because their parents and teachers have not yet learned how to cope with natural human instinct. At a time when sex education is a requirement in many schools, you would think this subject to be passé. But the recent success of a musical version of *Spring Awakening* on Broadway suggests that adolescent sexuality is still very much an important social issue.

Stylistically, the greatest influence on Wedekind was Georg Büchner, that strange postmodern prodigy of the early nineteenth-century Romantic stage, writing (in *Woyzeck*, for example) about the underside of human character when his German contemporaries were essentially preoccupied with outlandish heroic actions and flamboyant royal personages. If Büchner was Wedekind's immediate predecessor, his greatest follower was probably the early Bertolt Brecht of *Baal*, *In the Jungle of Cities*, and *Drums in the Night*, when Brecht's plays were still being lit by flashes of existential lightning rather than by political signal fires.

And of course, Wedekind's influence could later be found in the movies, in such films as *Zéro de Conduite*, *The Last Laugh*, and particularly *The Blue Angel*, which almost seems like a cinematic version of *Earth Spirit* with Marlene Dietrich in the part of Lulu. If his name is less familiar than his influence, that is because Benjamin Franklin Wedekind had the courage to write his own Declaration of Independence. As Yeats said of Jonathan Swift, "Imitate him if you dare. He served human liberty."

(2010)

August Strindberg

At first sight, August Strindberg would seem to be the most revolutionary spirit in modern theatre. Through his own inflammatory writings, he had a deep influence on such later theatrical "incendiaries" as Antonin Artaud, Jean Genet, and Edward Albee. In my opinion, the distinction of chief revolutionary must go to Ibsen, but Strindberg is certainly the more restless and experimental figure. Perpetually dissatisfied, perpetually reaching after shifting truths, he seems like a latter-day Faust with the unconscious as his laboratory, seeking the miracle of transmutation in the crucible of his tormented intellect.

The metaphor has not been carelessly chosen; the conversion of baser material into something higher, through the philosopher's stone of imagination, is the goal of all his activity, whether dramatic or nondramatic. Strindberg not only tries his hand at a great variety of dramatic styles, he also commits himself to a great variety of religious and political creeds. His literary work is one long autobiography, whether in the form of confessional novels, misogynistic short stories, revolutionary verses, scientific treatises, theatrical manifestoes, or short plays. More than any other dramatist in history, Strindberg wrote *himself*.

But that self changed radically over the years. At first he defined himself against Ibsen, convinced that this Norwegian "bluestocking" with his "Nora-cult" of feminism was spreading libels about his (Strindberg's) manhood. (Ibsen responded: "I cannot write a line without that madman standing and staring down at me with his mad eyes.") It is true that throughout his life Strindberg was subject to severe paranoid delusions. In the first macho stage of his career, he represents himself as a brutal naturalist often overcome (as in *The Father*) by the superior wiles of the female sex and its belief in supernatural powers. After a serious psychic breakdown in Paris, (known as his *Inferno* period), however, when he believed witches were trying to electrocute him through the walls of his room, he began to identify himself with the female cause, putting women figures at the suffering center of such plays as *Easter*, *A Dream Play*, and *The Ghost Sonata*. When he learned to control his misogyny in later years, and soften his resistance to the female principle, he began to face life with the quietism of a Buddhist saint, subordinating his defiant masculinity to the need for waiting, patience, expiation, and ordeals.

But it is impossible to capture Strindberg in a defining moment that is not immediately contradicted by a radical change in style and attack. His plays are the psychic biography of a man who suffered greatly and made others suffer greatly, which also have the continuing power to provoke and offend, and sometimes to heal.

(2010)

Tennessee Williams

Tennessee Williams was the first American playwright to bring a lyric sensibility to the stage. Eugene O'Neill had the makings of a poet, and Arthur Miller occasionally achieved a powerful urban music, particularly in *Death of a Salesman* (1949). But genuine dramatic poetry was virtually unknown on our stage until the advent of Thomas Lanier Williams III.

Williams had a remarkable ear for the florid vocabulary of the South. Because he was also influenced by such troubadours as Hart Crane and García Lorca and D. H. Lawrence, he had a natural affinity for metaphor and a way with form that was penetrating and unique.

The tension between a sensitive nature in a harsh environment was his great underlying theme: a conflict between what is delicate and poetic in American life and that which is unfeeling, brutalizing, and coarse. This, of course, is the basic conflict of *A Streetcar Named Desire* (1947) as reflected in the opposition between Blanche DuBois, an aristocratic Southern belle, and Stanley Kowalski, a crude Polish auto mechanic. But in Williams, this opposition is never simplistic. He knows there is decadence and corruption in the delicate Blanche, just as there is energy and life in the insensitive Stanley. Like Anton Chekhov, Williams loves cherry orchards but knows that they must have usefulness as well as beauty. That is why he celebrates his fallen heroines—Laura in *The Glass Menagerie* (1944), Alma in *Summer and Smoke* (1948), Catherine in *Suddenly Last Summer* (1959)—while recognizing how they contribute to their own destruction.

That destruction often comes by way of castration, whether physical or mental. Williams created a large number of women and men who are either lobotomized (like his sister was) or rendered impotent by the harsh paternalist values of the Southern Gothic culture. Chance Wayne in *Sweet*

Bird of Youth (1969), Brick in *Cat on a Hot Tin Roof* (1955), and Val Xavier in *Orpheus Descending* (1957) are instances of such characters. But he also created plenty of threatening males—Big Daddy in *Cat on a Hot Tin Roof* (1955), Boss Finley in *Sweet Bird of Youth* (1959), Jabe Torrance in *Orpheus Descending* (1957)—and occasional threatening females. The often ruthless matrons—Amanda Wingfield in *The Glass Menagerie* (1944), Lady Torrance in *Orpheus Descending* (1957), Alexandra Del Lago in *Sweet Bird of Youth* (1969)—love their men so long as they can control and dominate them.

Blanche DuBois insists that she must have magic. The art of Tennessee Williams, which continues to be unparalleled, provides that magic without losing touch with reality.

(2010)

August Wilson

August Wilson would seem to have sprung full-blown from the head of some African godhead, but actually the seeds of his theatrical development had been planted in the radical years following the assassinations of Martin Luther King, Jr. and Malcolm X. First, LeRoi Jones (later Amiri Baraka) contributed a couple of inflammatory plays off-Broadway, notably *Dutchman* and *The Slave* in 1964, which signaled the presence of a rebellious new black voice on stage. Then, James Baldwin, essentially a novelist and an essayist, demonstrated with *Blues for Mister Charlie* (1964) that he had playwriting instincts, too, with roots in the blues. And then a large number of African American dramatists, among them Lonne Elder, OyomO, Ed Bullins, and others—some trained at the Yale Drama School and most operating out of Joe Papp's Public Theatre—began to investigate a culture that for years had been kept in the shadows. (So did Spike Lee with his powerful movies.)

But nothing had prepared this country for the entrance of August Wilson—born Frederick August Kittel, Jr. in the Hill District of Pittsburgh. Beginning as a poet, inspired by Bessie Smith and the racking pain of the blues, Wilson delivered his first major work with *Ma Rainey's Black Bottom* in 1984. Other plays had preceded it, but this Broadway hit was the first to receive national attention, and Wilson was soon embarked upon a ten play series of work, called *The Pittsburgh Cycle*, designed to celebrate the black experience in every decade of the twentieth century. These works varied in quality from the highly charged, poetic *Joe Turner is Come and Gone* to the somewhat anemic *Radio Golf*, but it was an incredibly ambitious effort, matched only in size and audacity by Eugene O'Neill's projected (but unfinished) cycle of plays about the entire American historical experience. O'Neill had intended an eleven-play chronicle of an Irish American family. He only wrote two—*A Touch of the Poet* and the unfinished *More Stately Mansions*. Wilson finished his cycle of African American life after ten plays.

As the country's leading black playwright, collecting a number of Tonys and Pulitzer Prizes, Wilson began to function as a spokesman for the African American theatre as a whole. In a highly publicized event at Town Hall, he and I debated his conviction that black actors not be allowed to perform in plays by white playwrights, such as Shakespeare or Beckett, and that white directors refrain from staging plays by black playwrights. Wilson also criticized the current process—of which he was perhaps the greatest beneficiary—of cycling black plays through "white" theatres instead of originating them in black-run institutions.

Contradictory positions such as these were related, in the opinion of some, to the fact that Wilson rarely acknowledged the truth of his own origins—that he was half white himself, his father having been an immigrant German baker. In a well-publicized speech, he asserted that the "ground on which I stand" was the deck of a seventeenth-century African slave ship, when it was actually also the floor of a twentieth-century German strudel shop. If Wilson had lived, I feel confident he would have reexamined these inconsistencies, including his seeming call for self-imposed segregation, and evolved a whole new postracial take on relations between the black and white people of America. Alas, he died too soon, but not before creating a body of work that was electrifying in its plotting, majestic in its sweep, syncopated in its rhythms, powerful in its characters, and awe-inspiring in its ambitions.

(2010)

3

Commemorative Passages

F. Murray Abraham

In 1984, F. Murray Abraham won an Academy Award for poisoning Wolfgang Amadeus Mozart. Not unusual. For years, Hollywood has been awarding Oscars for eating off the remains of great classical artists. Tchaikovsky, in particular, was often cannibalized in Westerns, especially during scenes that featured covered wagons rolling toward the Western sun. But Murray's Oscar was the first time, to my knowledge, that a great actor was honored for murdering one of the greatest icons of Western culture.

Today, Murray is being celebrated as something of an icon himself. One of the most distinguished American actors of the past half century, and also one of the most intelligent, F. Murray Abraham has always been known for his almost quixotic devotion to the stage.

There is little in his past history to lead us to predict such a passion. Born in El Paso to parents of Syrian extraction (his father, Fahid, was a cantor in a Syrian Church), Murray served an apprenticeship as a gang member before discovering the even more illicit attractions of acting on the stage. That early experience comes through quite terrifyingly in his impersonation of Omar Suarez in *Scarface*, with his hooded eyes and menacing sneer. And as a matter of fact, during a recent rehearsal at the Classic Stage Company, he called on his old expertise by trading some blows with a thief who had come to rob his dressing room.

Murray matriculated at a college that was later to become the University of Texas at El Paso, and before long he was in New York studying acting with the great Uta Hagen and supporting himself through such TV commercials as the Fruit of the Loom where he played the voice of a talking bunch of grapes.

Amadeus aside, it as a Shakespearean actor that Murray has most distinguished himself. He is surely among the best of that Olympian breed now appearing on the American stage. In a 2007 doubleheader, he played the roles of Shylock in *Merchant* and Barabas in *The Jew of Malta* side by side for Jeffrey Horowitz's Theatre for a New Audience. (Murray's triumphant Shylock was reprised the next year in Boston at ArtsEmerson, newly under the directorship of Rob Orchard.) In 1991, he did a stunning Lear for us at the American Repertory Theatre, playing him like a homeless Bowery derelict, too weak to carry the dead Cordelia onto the stage (and solving this knotty portage problem for all time by schlepping his daughter's corpse onstage by her arm). His Pozzo in Mike Nichols's *Waiting for Godot* at Lincoln Center is still remembered as the centerpiece of that production. And I shall personally never forget his Doctor Astrov in Andrei Şerban's production of *Uncle Vanya*, pulling at his face hairs and saying, "I hate this moustache."

Murray is sometimes known to have a fiery temperament. But he is a fond father and a warm and loyal friend, and he has been a devoted husband to his delightful wife, Kate, for forty-eight years. He is a man whose generous heart beats in his reverberant voice. F. Murray Abraham may have killed Mozart, but he has brought to birth hundreds of great characters during his forty-year career upon the American stage, most recently a CIA chief in *Homeland*. Let us all celebrate this protean theatre artist.

Robert Woodruff

Few would dispute the fact that Robert Woodruff is one of the most visionary artists in the American theatre. Where there might be some disagreement is over exactly who this visionary artist actually is. Start with his name. Some people were accustomed to calling him Woody. Others were used to calling him Bob. The man himself will tell you he prefers to be called Robert. Does this suggest that Robert Woodruff periodically undergoes some kind of mutation, that this hugely gifted, transforming artist might be in the process of transforming himself?

Clearly, his changing identity over forty years as a professional director reflects not so much transmutations in character as alterations in aesthetic, possibly influenced by Robert's many geographical and professional pilgrimages.

He was born in Brooklyn—birthplace of artists and derelicts, of BAM and the Bums, and in process of becoming the working home of a great peripatetic institution, the Theatre for a New Audience. He quickly relocated, like the Brooklyn Dodgers, to the West, where he founded the Eureka Theatre in San Francisco. Not long after, this budding genius did a number of premieres written by another budding genius, the young Sam Shepard, both in California and New York. Woody, as he was then called, was responsible for staging *Curse of the Starving Class*, *Buried Child*, *Tongues* and *Savage Love*, and *True West*, and probably could have spent the rest of his life as a director fastened to the work of leading American playwrights.

True West, which he directed at the Magic Theatre in San Francisco with Peter Coyote and Jim Haynie, came to New York in 1980. Joe Papp invited Robert to restage it at the Public with a cast that now was starring Tommy Lee Jones and Peter Boyle. This occasion led to the first of a few famous kerfuffles when Woody (I mean Robert) quit the production and Papp took over, for reasons I have never fully understood. Shepard hated the project without ever having seen it. Woodruff says he left during previews because the play simply wasn't working. But despite the fact that he had repudiated his own production, Robert had left a vivid imprint upon it. I saw it at the Public when it first opened, and, unaware that so many thought it was being ruined by movie stars, gave it a rave review. By 1978, when Robert directed his last Shepard production, *Buried Child* at Theatre for the New City in New York, I was in my next to last year with the Yale Repertory Theatre, competing with Robert for the privilege of premiering Sam's plays.

I didn't have the sense to invite Robert Woodruff to join our company until I had started the American Repertory Theatre at Harvard. By this time, having permanently moved East, Woody had metamorphosed into Robert, no longer the deferential directorial channel for Shepard or for any other single American playwright, but rather an authentic European auteur, one who wore a pony tail, chewed gum, and looked as if he had spent his life smoking Gauloises in existential French cafes. It was Woodruff who turned *The Comedy of Errors* into a juggling exercise at Lincoln Center starring The Flying Karamazov Brothers. And it was Woodruff who staged a dazzling production of *Baal* at Anne Bogart's Trinity Rep in 1990. By this time, Robert had obviously fallen under the influence of Bertolt Brecht; during the same period I was falling under the influence of Robert Woodruff. But he was developing a distinctly personal style, pulsing with feverish visual imagery. Robert was using the stage in a manner it had rarely been used before—as a palette for painting action, as a metaphorical medium.

I asked him to the ART where, in a very brief moment of time, he turned out three outstanding productions, Brecht's *In the Jungle of Cities*, Charles L. Mee's *Full Circle* (a loose adaptation of *The Caucasian Chalk Circle*), and Shakespeare's *Richard II*. Just as Brecht had once transformed Shakespeare's *Coriolanus* into an adjunct masterpiece called *Coriolan*, so Robert was reconstructing works by Shakespeare and Brecht into totally original creations, true to the text, yet utterly original, flashing with satanic imagery, yet always maintaining their flawed humanity.

His first two Brecht productions at the ART won him Boston's top theatre prize—the Elliot Norton Award. Only his Shakespeare aroused any controversy. Somewhat in the manner of the off-Broadway director played by Paul Benedict in *The Goodbye Girl*, who forces Richard Dreyfus to play the hump-backed Richard III not as a British king but as a Greenwich Village queen, Robert collaborated with Tommy Derrah to turn Richard II into a flamboyant transvestite, first seen applying paint to his features in front of a dressing room mirror before descending a huge staircase in the manner of Gloria Swanson telling Cecil B. DeMille that she is ready for her close-up.

This is the production that sent John Simon raging out of the theatre after the first intermission to write a nauseated denunciation. Years later, having forgotten that review, I stupidly asked John and Robert to appear together on a panel concerned with transformative directing, where Simon repeated with great gusto his vituperative comments about Robert's Richard II. Upon being questioned as to how he could review the whole production having only seen half of it, Simon replied with the same appetitive metaphors he had used in his review: "If the main course is disgusting, I don't have to stay for the whole meal." What he preferred, apparently, was to ruin the appetites of everybody else in the restaurant.

Actually, a number of discriminating diners enjoyed the five-course repast that Robert served up in *Richard II*. It constituted an explicit expression of what was already implicit in the play. Robert's *Richard* opened during my next-to-last season at the ART, and when I finished my tenure there, Robert seemed the sensible choice to succeed me. Apart from a Brooklyn birthplace and the same first names, we shared pretty much the same aesthetic, the same taste in actors, and the same passion for training. (By this time Robert was on the faculty of Columbia's School of the Arts, turning out more bold young directors.) Indeed, there are few people in the American theatre with whom I feel such a common identity—another is Robert's mentor, Jeffrey Horowitz. But the thing that ultimately persuaded me to propose his name as ART's artistic leader was the uncommon generosity he displayed toward other artists in the theatre, particularly auteur directors. That generosity, so essential to anybody heading an artistic institution, is not a quality often found in our profession.

The fact is that Robert's five-year appointment at Harvard proved a little rocky. The productions all possessed a high integrity, and all were stunningly produced, both by Robert and the brilliant directors he invited to share the ART stage with him. But I think it is fair to say that not many of these productions were guided by the pleasure principle.

Robert was more committed to fulfilling his bold uncompromising artistic vision than appealing to what the critic Walter Kerr once called "the hearts and minds of the folks out front." (Kerr coined that phrase in the act of panning the Broadway production of *Waiting for Godot* and scolding

Samuel Beckett for being out of touch with popular audiences.) But contrary to the opinion of not a few detractors, Robert had no desire to alienate audiences either. Rather, he assumed that the folks out front would embrace the same kind of things that pleased him.

It may have been that Robert had an overly exalted estimation of popular taste. To give you an example, after describing his controversial concept of the first act of the play at a production meeting for *Richard III*, Robert said about the set, "And then everything goes away." "Including the audience," I quipped. Shocked, Robert replied that I was underestimating my own subscribers. (But I wasn't. As predicted, not a few of them went away after the first act.)

Another example: during one of his seasons, Bill Camp and Elizabeth Marvel, both of who had acted with the ART resident company, expressed a desire to perform together under Robert's direction in Molière's *Le Misanthrope*, which aside from being unquestionably brilliant would have attracted large satisfied audiences. But in the same slot, Robert was also considering Racine's *Britannicus*, an obscure play about an obscure Roman Emperor, obscure to the point of invisibility to most of our subscribers. All of us kept our peace for fear that expressing any enthusiasm for the Molière would encourage Robert to do the Racine. Robert chose *Britannicus* anyway, losing Bill and Elizabeth in the process. He gave it a splendid production but one that was hardly designed to start a box-office stampede. Other brilliant ART productions from this period similarly attracted both praise from critics and defections from those subscribers who hadn't gotten the message that Robert's choices were paying them the highest compliment.

In bygone days when more generous financial support from public and private sources helped relieve the pressure on the box office, this would not have been such a problem. In my second year as artistic director of the ART, for example, the year of Lee Breuer's *Lulu*, we lost half of our subscription base and survived. But doing this kind of uncompromising material in a sour financial climate caused Robert to commit one of the mortal sins against Harvard's theology; he ran a deficit. To compensate for losses at the box office, the ART drew down a larger percentage of interest income from the endowment than was authorized, thus committing another deadly Harvard sin: failing to accelerate the growth of departmental funds. Having become aware that Robert Woodruff was not going to inflate the bottom line with Broadway-bound musicals or not-for-profit populism or that franchise approach to production circulation I have elsewhere called McTheatre, Harvard let him go.

It was a shocking decision, not unlike the treatment of Anne Bogart at the Trinity Rep and JoAnne Akalaitis at the Public and most recently Kate Whoriskey at Seattle's Intiman, because it signaled the decline and fall of the experimental not-for-profit theatre. But dismaying as this may have seemed at the time, I think it was the best thing that could have happened to Robert. (It certainly helped me assuage some of the guilt I was feeling about having exposed him to such torment in the first place.) Not having his contract renewed by Harvard freed Robert from onerous administrative duties and allowed him to turn his entire attention over to creating theatre art. He was able to resume his teaching, first at the Yale Drama School and then at Columbia where he trained some excellent student directors and where, along with the plays he has been directing for Theatre for a New Audience, some of his most compelling work has appeared. His triumphant adaptation at the Yale Rep of Dostoyevsky's *Notes from the Underground*, with Bill Camp as actor and collaborator, transferred successfully to Theatre for a New Audience, and his recently-opened Yale production of Ingmar Bergman's

Autumn Sonata, wracked with grief and recrimination, reveals how well he wears the cap of a post-modern European auteur director.

And he has had the great good luck to have been associated with Theatre for a New Audience, which is among a handful of American institutions willing to support his vision. Along with its co-partnered productions, such as *Notes from Underground* and *Orpheus X*, Jeffrey Horowitz's brave theatre has staged Robert's *The Changeling* and two Edward Bond productions, among them *Saved*, perhaps the most harrowing rendering of a Bond work I have ever seen. For those of you who don't know the play, I will simply say that it features the stoning by some particularly brutal London hoods of an infant in his cradle. How's that for pandering to the pleasure principle?

So Woody, Bob, Robert, whatever you prefer to be called at the moment, thank you for having distinguished the American theatre with your remarkable vision, boldness, and integrity—qualities that this award from the Theatre for a New Audience has engraved not in stone but in precious metal.

(2010)

John Douglas Thompson

In the first appearance of John Douglas Thompson on the ART stage in 1995, he was gorgeously attired as the French ambassador in the Ron Daniels production of *Henry V*. It was one of the rare times when a man inside a costume was more resplendent than his clothes. We had stolen John from the Trinity Rep. (Oskar Eustis, I hope you have forgiven us.) But after *Henry V*, John proceeded to play nine more roles for us: Polixenes in *The Winter's Tale*, Creon in *Antigone*, the Cook in *Mother Courage*, Duperret in *Marat/Sade*, Fyodor in *The Idiots Karamazov*, and a number of smaller parts, including one in Charles Mee's *Full Circle*, a modern adaptation of

The Caucasian Chalk Circle in which our own Cherry Jones played Grusha, that I still can't get out of mind.

After that, of course, came his magnificent Othello in 2001. It was a role he had already played at Trinity, where he did some of his actor training, and he was destined to play it many times again, notably with Shakespeare & Company and Theatre for a New Audience. He became, in fact, so closely identified with the Moor that I wouldn't be surprised if he actually believed his own stories about the Anthropophagi and the men whose heads do grow beneath their shoulders.

At the ART, he played Othello with Tommy Derrah as Iago and Karen MacDonald as Emilia. We didn't make the assignment easy for him. First of all, his Desdemona, Mirjana Jokovic, was a Yugoslav, beautiful and gifted, whose English was heavily accented. And second of all, his director, Yuri Yuremin, was a Russian, bravely experimental, whose English was severely limited. John must have thought he had entered a Slavic centrifuge. Heavily indebted to Stanislavski, Yuremin apparently believed that asides and soliloquies were unrealistic, and since Iago spends a lot of his time making evil confessions to the audience, Tommy's part was cut almost in half. So, by the way, was Karen's Emilia. I was very fond of Yuri, but it had become very clear that he really wanted to direct another play, preferably one with a fourth wall. I had no other choice but to replace him with the late David Wheeler, who restored all the cuts, while Yuri was given credit for his concept and his *mise-en-scène*.

Throughout this creative ordeal, John remained calm, gen-erous, and uncomplaining and, as a matter of fact, delivered one of the most powerful performances of the year in any theatre. But another reason he is receiving this award is not only because he is an exemplary artist, but because he is a truly special individual. Indeed, there may not be a more decent human being working in theatre today. His smile is as broad as his face, and you can't greet him without hugging him. Having reached these shores by way of Bath, England, where he was born, and Montreal where his family emigrated, he moved to this country in the mid-eighties to study business at Le Moyne College and to become a travelling computer salesman when he graduated. All those who love the theatre should be grateful that he soon lost that job, abandoned electronics, started studying acting and doing repertory, and becoming such a highly regarded professional that even *The New York Times* took notice, writing: "There may be no better classical actor working in the New York theatre right now."

Yes, he has done the obligatory television roles and movies, but he has always remained faithful to the classics—and more importantly, to classical companies. That is why he is such a supreme candidate for an award that goes to an artist who has made supreme contributions to the resident theatre movement, and it is why it gives me such personal pride to personally hand it to my dear friend, John Douglas Thompson.

(2010)

Oskar Eustis

The American Repertory Theatre has chosen February 14 as the date of its 2011 Gala, but we don't need a holiday pretext to send Valentine's Day cards to Oskar Eustis. The recipient of this year's Robert Brustein Award is already universally beloved. Shakespeare's Falstaff says that he is not only witty in himself, but the cause that wit is in others. Oskar Eustis is that rare breed of artist, not only talented in himself but the facilitator of talent in others. He has been lucky enough to share those gifts with a truly delightful family—among them, Laurie, his creative, gracious, and handsome wife, equally effective as a mother and as a professional, and their gifted son, Jack.

Oskar's selfless nature has led him to devote most of his creative energies to the development of other talents. Joe Papp, his predecessor at the Public, used to feature what he called "hunchback plays" in his scheduling, meaning new works that cried out to be seen, despite their sometimes visible defects. Oskar has expanded the Public Theatre's experimental daring with his Under the Radar series, billed as "a festival tracking theater from around the world." It is a scheduling challenge that would send the stationmaster of Pennsylvania Station into breakdown; on one Sunday in January alone, the Public featured fifteen different offerings from all over the map in the course of a single day.

Oskar not only identifies, invites, and restages work from other venues. He discovers and develops original work too. As dramaturge, resident director, and then artistic director of California's Eureka Theatre until 1989, he famously commissioned and then helped to shape a play by another recent ART Award winner, Tony Kushner's *Angels in America*. Oskar also became one of the first directors of *Millennium Approaches* when it opened at the Eureka Theatre, before he and the play moved to the Mark Taper Auditorium. Thus he has been responsible for some of the most epic American plays of our time—not only Tony Kushner's universally acclaimed two-part *Angels in America*, but Robert Schenkkan's Pulitzer Prize–winning nine-act *The Kentucky Cycle* as well.

Let me tell you something about Oskar I have never revealed before. When I retired from the artistic directorship of the ART in 2001, Oskar was running our sister theatre in Providence, the Trinity Rep, where I got to see some wonderful theatre and eat some fattening Italian meals with him and Laurie preceding visits to his shows. Now I yield to very few in my admiration for Robert Woodruff, but it was Oskar who was my first choice to succeed me at the ART, and not just because we shared the same taste in restaurants. Harvard made him the offer and Oskar turned it down. His reason? He had not yet succeeded in linking his training conservatory, the Trinity's Consortium for Professional Theatre Training, with the academic programs of Brown University.

One could only admire Oskar's dedication to a larger idea than his own career. Indeed, he was demonstrating the very artistic selflessness that had made him so appealing in the first place. Oskar has always been dedicated to helping theatre artists grow and develop. And when he went to the Public, he was in an even better position to pursue his interest in eclectic programming—from *Hair*, the international musical hit, which our own Diane Paulus turned into such a rousing evocation of radical America's hirsute past, to all the rich and diverse offerings that are currently bringing such variety to Lafayette Street.

As you may know, artistic directors don't often have the time to direct many plays. But a week ago, I was privileged to see a show at the Public staged by Oskar, namely Rinne Groff's *Compulsion*. A drama about Meyer Levin's obsessive effort to win respect for his own version of the Anne Frank story in the face of commercial, ideological, and personal prejudices, *Compulsion* proved a compelling journey into pathological breakdown, enriched by the substitution of expressive puppets for all but three of the actors in the cast. What a shrewd budgetary decision! But aside from showcasing Oskar's fiscal responsibility, and his considerable directorial talents, the evening displayed many of his humanistic concerns—the way people betray themselves through obsessive behavior, the growing rightward political drift of our country, and the hope for national redemption through the innocence of children.

Oskar is an old-fashioned Leftie who, Wikipedia informs us, changed his first name from Paul in order to reflect affinities with the German socialist culture he loved, especially that of

Karl Marx and Bertolt Brecht. But Oskar is also the first name of the great German actor Oskar Werner and of the great German martyr Oskar Schindler and it is that rare blend of art and humanity—I am tempted to call it "Oskarism"—that is being honored tonight. Unlike the more practical professions, art is often dedicated to enlarging rather than diminishing what it means to be human. It tries to bring light into dark interiors in order to illuminate the human heart, yes, but also to suggest that our experience is ruled not just by Thanatos, or death, but by a passionate life figure called Eros as well. And that is how I often think of Oskar, as a benevolent American grizzly bear, whose hug brings warmth and reinforcement rather than pain and suffocation, the only kind of bear you would ever want to hug back. Oskar, come and exchange some hugs.

(2012)

Carmen De Lavallade

Carmen De Lavallade—her very name rings like a bell. But how can one invoke, aside from repeating those mantric syllables, the spiritual and physical beauty of this exquisite creature? Carmen has always been the amethyst in the crown of our art. During a time when balletic swans are winning Academy Awards by mutilating themselves with glass shards, Carmen always won her own awards by virtue of her grace, her good nature, her gentleness, and her generosity. She not only made the world a gift of her dancing talent, she passed it on through her teaching. And as a result, countless young students still carry their experiences of Carmen in their bones.

Carmen first came to us at Yale in the 1980s, as a movement instructor, her hair pulled back in a severe bun, dazzling in a leotard, her Creole features a model of perfection; dozens of theatre students in dozens of schools have since profited by her patience and expertise. But it was not long before Carmen began taking on acting assignments, growing in size from role to role. One hears little debate over the fact that her crowning achievement was Titania in Alvin Epstein's *A Midsummer Night's Dream*. (Joe Grifasi graced that production as well, playing an addled and hilarious Thisbe.) Watching her slither down a splendidly dangerous wooden scoop, designed by Tony Straiges, like some angelic reptile, her lovely fingers pointing toward the outstretched hand of Christopher Lloyd's Oberon, was to watch an indelible image that has never faded from the mind. "Fairies away," she would command after one of their more vigorous arguments, "I shall chide downright if I longer stay." Carmen could chide down right, down left, or even down center, if the staging demanded it, without ever seeming to lose her balance or grace. She has always been the most generous of creatures, the most loving of friends, and like our old comrade dear Joe Grifasi, the recorder and amanuensis of every formal occasion, whether births, birthdays, marriages, or deaths. Paths would cross, divide, suspend, and careen in separate directions. But Carmen never forgot that our associations were not only professional; they were personal and, therefore, never to be neglected. Has she ever forgotten your birthday? She has never forgotten one of mine. And now that she has reached the age of eighty, we must make certain never again to forget hers, but to commemorate the three or four decades she has left with her family, her friends, and her profession, with the reverence this remarkable artist deserves.

Hail to you, Carmen De Lavallade, with all the passion of our collective love and admiration. Dancing, singing, acting, or simply being, you have exhilarated your friends and left the world a happier, more ravishing, and more bewitching place. "Fairies away. We shall weep downright if we longer stay." But there are multitudes of loving colleagues and former students who will weep downright if you go away.

(2012)

Christopher Durang

I once described Christopher Durang as an angelic choir boy with arsenic leeching through his fingertips. At the time, I was trying to characterize a unique American writer (he also happened to be a former student and longtime friend) who, professionally, came on like Lucifer throwing matches at the world, but who, in person, was always tender, soft-spoken, and courteous.

I now think I was also trying to describe Durang's divided self. One senses his alienation in every word he writes, but he is not by nature a rebel. What he has been rejecting is a system that powerfully dominated his childhood years. Clearly, an inordinate number of Christopher Durang's plays have been inspired by a loss of faith in traditional values. He abandoned his trust in the possibility of happy families when he saw his alcoholic father abusing his miscarrying mother; he lost his enthusiasm for patriotic affirmations when he watched the land of his birth embark on brutal imperial adventures; he lost his belief in equality under the law in the face of discrimination against blacks, gays, and lesbians; and he lost his religious faith when he realized that the heavens do not often reward virtue or punish sin.

This is not to say that Durang is merely a predictable iconoclast or knee-jerk anarchist. The character of Angry Black Woman in *Media Amok*, for example, reveals that he not only can satirize people who think in stereotypes, but those who behave like stereotypes as well. But underlying Durang's sometimes vitriolic satire lies a painful religious apostasy. Reared as a pious Roman Catholic, Durang gradually learned that God doesn't often answer prayers. ("He does," argues Sister Mary Ignatius, "but sometimes the answer is no.") And God certainly doesn't seem very eager to reward the innocent. ("I don't think God punishes people for specific things," says a character in *The Marriage of Bette and*

Boo. "I think he punishes people in general, for no reason.")
As a result of this discovery, Durang's early Christian piety
eventually gave way to a profound disenchantment, his lost
innocence pushed aside by a lacerating sense of the absurd.
("I don't believe in God anymore," says a character in *Beyond
Therapy*, "I believe in bran cereal.") This kind of unexpected
juxtaposition, between the metaphysical and the mundane,
provides the inspiration for much of Durang's comedy, which
manages to be outrageously funny precisely because it springs
from a basis of pain and regret.

The same kind of division can be found in Durang's
simultaneous embrace of high art and popular culture. His
greatest artistic influences have often been avant-garde icons
such as Ionesco, Beckett, and Orton. But his style also owes
a considerable debt to Broadway musicals and to the gilded
Hollywood of the 1930s and 1940s—a passion fully exploited
in his *History of American Film*. It is hardly unusual for serious
artists to borrow from popular culture. The plays of both
T. S. Eliot and e. e. cummings show the influence of
vaudeville and the music hall, just as much of Brecht's work
finds its roots in Berlin cabaret. *Waiting for Godot* could
hardly have been written in the same manner without the
examples of Chaplin and Keaton. Ionesco owes a huge debt
to Groucho Marx.

So, by the way, does Durang, and he may owe a few Euros
to Monty Python as well. To take just one example of his
antic juxtapositions, allow me to cite his first professional
production (cowritten with Albert Innaurato) called *The
Idiots Karamazov*, produced at the Yale Repertory Theatre
in 1974 when Durang was still a student at the School of
Drama. Durang belonged to a legendary student body, which
included (to name but a handful) Wendy Wasserstein, Ted
Tally, William Hauptman, Robert Auletta, Sigourney Weaver,
Eric Ellice, Steve Rowe, Kate McGregor Stewart, Christine

Estabrook, and Meryl Streep. Durang's art at that time had been partly honed at the Yale Cabaret, often performing with his close friend, Sigourney Weaver, a collaboration that would long outlast their student days. The compressed, staccato influence of cabaret was certainly on view in the opening moments of *The Idiots Karamazov*, when Alyosha, Ivan, and Dimitri rush on stage to sing, "Oh, we got to get to Moscow," as if they were Chekhov's Three Sisters performing the opening number of a Frank Loesser musical. By the time the play was over, the stage was littered with the detritus of Western literature.

Durang later went on to satirize sadistic nuns (*Sister Mary Agnes Explains It All to You*), then both the Vietnam War and those who wrote conscience-stricken plays about it (*The Vietnamization of New Jersey*), psychotic psychoanalysts (*Beyond Therapy*), mismatched unions (*The Marriage of Bette and Boo*), mindless television (*Media Amok*), brainless childrearing (*Baby With the Bathwater*), shy homosexual serial killers (*Betty's Summer Vacation*), and almost any other contemporary lunacy you can think of. He had become the voice of an outraged, bemused, and stoical humanity, inveighing against all forms of lapsarian behavior—as well as an absolutely invaluable antidote to our national pathology.

(2012)

Philip Roth

Philip Roth, who has just turned eighty, has been writing novels, stories, essays, autobiographical books, and other species of cultural provocation for over half a century now. Claiming that literary composition is a form of mental anguish and physical agony (he writes standing up to spare a bad back), he has announced that his last book, *Nemesis*, will be his last book. Nobody wants to believe him. How can we watch without protest our greatest living writer withdraw into silence?

Roth's first story, published in *The New Yorker* in 1959, was "Defender of the Faith" (reprinted soon after in his collection, *Goodbye Columbus*). Its frankness about Jewish tribal behavior predictably created the earliest of his many stormy confrontations with the Jewish establishment, one of whose members threatened him with medieval retribution. It is doubtful whether Roth ever consciously intended to kindle extremist fires. But his compulsion to tell the truth, regardless of wounded sensibilities, made him born to trouble, as the sparks fly upward. Some of this history has been chronicled in the first of what will doubtless be numerous celebrations of Roth's achievement, a new PBS documentary called *Philip Roth: Unmasked* on *American Masters*. (I don't doubt some wag, citing *Portnoy's Complaint*, will rechristen the program *American Masturbators*.) Another celebration is taking place in Newark, a huge birthday party, during which a square will be renamed after one of the city's most famous former strollers. I remember how, when Roth was visiting his ailing father in Florida, he wistfully pointed out the Miami avenue that had been named for Isaac Bashevis Singer. You've got your own now, Phillie.

I've known Philip Roth now for almost all of his writing life, beginning in the sixties, when he used to eat a lot of dinners at the New York apartment of my late wife, Norma, and myself. One of those culinary adventures we had scheduled on the night of the Great Northeast Blackout of 1965. Although the phone system was down, all the guests correctly guessed that the dinner had been cancelled. Not Phil. He arrived just on time, having solved the dead subway problem by walking up two miles of dark streets and the dead elevator problem by walking up eight flights of stairs. He had a metaphorical napkin tucked under his chin, so naturally we were eager to feed him.

A few years later, he and I happened to be together at Yaddo (a writer's colony near Saratoga), where all of the guests, not me least of all, were eager to finish our daily regimen of coffee, sandwiches, literary labors, and silence in order to enjoy Roth's delicious stream of standup after dinner. One night, as he was performing those verbal acrobatics, his spritz was interrupted by a phone call. When he returned to the dining room, his brow was dark. He told us that he had to leave immediately. Only later did I learn that a friend of his had attempted suicide and that he had gone to lend his support at the bedside. It was not long before he began to add his support to a host of imperiled middle-European writers.

One of Phil's best comic turns was at my expense and took place on Martha's Vineyard during one of his many visits there. Our mutual friend, Bill Styron, had recently sent me what he considered to be an amusing photo, taken many years past, of my son Daniel (6) and his daughter Alexandra (4) roped together back to back in chairs by Bill's mischievous son, Tommy (8). It happened that week that my television needed fixing, and when the repairman left, the photo was also gone. Within hours, I was visited by two detectives who wanted to know if I enjoyed abusing children. I did what I could to persuade them of my spotless character, even calling Alexandra to have her confirm the facts and thus somehow managed to retrieve my photograph and my reputation. Well, not quite. After a dinner party at the Styrons that evening, Phil put me on the stand and prosecuted me remorselessly for child abuse.

Admiring his ear for American speech, I worked very hard to squeeze a play out of Phil after I went to Yale in 1966 to start the Yale Repertory Theatre. He wrote one full-length piece for us, which he then decided not to submit, so I satisfied my Roth needs with a short satire (from *Our Gang*) about the Nixon Impeachment called "The President Addresses the Nation." In this, Nixon recognizes the Congressional right to impeach him—and then refuses to leave office ("That's not the kind of president you elected me to be.") We included this pitch-perfect skit as the final offering in an evening called *Watergate Classics*. I played Nixon, ending the speech with hunched shoulder V-waves to my imaginary admirers. The National Guard, with bayonets drawn, took up positions in the house as the audience filed out.

Phil's other association with the Yale Rep came about after he had married the actress Claire Bloom. Spending much of his time in London, he devoted himself to her career, helping to write adaptations of television and stage works (mostly Chekhov) in which she was appearing at the time. After they moved back to the United States, and around the time of their divorce, Claire played a few roles with our company (most notably Mary Tyrone in *A Long Day's Journey into Night* and Madame Ranevsky in *The Cherry Orchard*). Phil had been a constant presence and tireless advisor, a caretaker of her talents until they parted in 1995.

After this painful divorce, Phil became a lot more reclusive, spending most of his time in a house he had bought in Cornwall, Connecticut. A number of physical complaints, however, not unusual among geezers like us, have forced him now to spend the winter months in his New York apartment. There he exercises, corresponds, naps, and no doubt stares at his typewriter with scorn and derision. One advantage of his determination to retire from literature is that a private man accustomed to avoiding interviews and feature stories because they interfere too much with his writing is now destined to become a much more public figure. Also, let us hope, a more universally celebrated one. Note to the Nobel Prize Committee: Now vee may perhaps to begin? Yes?

(2013)

David Wheeler

Our beloved David Wheeler was scheduled to receive the Robert Brustein Award in early February. He died in early January. It was the only time I can remember when David failed to show up for an appointment.

When the ART arrived in Boston in 1979, David Wheeler was one of the first Boston artists to show up and bring us friendly greetings. He was already a legend in the area, having founded the groundbreaking Theatre Company of Boston, which he led from 1963 to 1975. In that venue, David directed over eighty plays, including ten by Pinter, seven by Brecht, five by Albee, nine by Beckett, and two by O'Neill, as well as numerous works by new playwrights such as Ed Bullins, Jeffrey Bush, John Hawkes, Adrienne Kennedy, and Sam Shepard.

He was not only responsive to young writers. He also launched the careers of a number of actors—notably our late, much missed company member Paul Benedict, Larry Bryggman, John Cazale, Stockard Channing, Blythe Danner, Robert DeNiro, Robert Duvall, Hector Elizondo, Spalding Gray, Paul Guilfoyle, Dustin Hoffman, Al Pacino, Jon Voight, Ralph Waite, and James Woods. On Broadway, he had directed *Richard III* with Al Pacino and *The Basic Training of Pavlo Hummel*, for which Pacino won the Tony for Best Actor. In Paris, he directed the French premiere of Edward Albee's *The Zoo Story*. And his 1990 movie, *The Local Stigmatic* (also with Al Pacino), was presented at the Montreal Film Festival and screened at the Whitney Museum and MOMA. David's long relationship with Pacino suggests that he was a director in which an actor could put absolute trust.

With spectacles on nose and pouch on side, wearing a turtleneck shirt, and sporting a David Niven moustache, David looked a bit like an actor himself. He was a graduate of Harvard, where he returned to teach during his ART years, but he always held his learning lightly. Most attractive of all was his good nature—modest, generous, gracious, and warmhearted. I never saw him ruffled. And he managed to soften the most fractious of temperaments with a gentle stroke on the back.

Alas, his company having dissolved, David was theatrically homeless until we arrived. He could have moved to New York. But I'm awfully glad he didn't. As our resident director for the next twenty or so years, he created some of the ART's most distinguished and available work.

But to tell you the truth, I never understood how David got his results. I remember, for example, during rehearsals for Shaw's *Misalliance*, a scene wasn't working and soap bubbles were beginning to form. When I raised a peep, David, ever jaunty, ever jolly, replied, "I know how to fix it," and promptly asked Jeremy Geidt to move from his chair stage right to another stage left. And you know what? It worked! The production developed a new sparkle and went on to become one of the most popular shows in ART history. Only David knew the secret of how a simple stage direction could transform an entire evening.

At the ART, David was responsible not only for all those wonderful Shaws and wondrous Becketts, but productions of plays by Don DeLillo, Harold Pinter, Steve Martin, Howard Korder, Sam Shepard, Anton Chekhov, William Shakespeare, and me. How did I get in such company? Because of David. I will always be personally indebted to him for his staging of *Nobody Dies on Friday*, about Lee Strasberg and Marilyn Monroe, along with practically all of the ten-minute skits I had been writing the last ten years for the Boston Playwrights Marathon. Working with David gave me insight into why so many actors adored him. He never waved the wand of the auteur, never wielded the whip of the tyrant, and never put anything heavy on the shoulders of others. He was always the modest and friendly support of his artistic collaborators, quietly assisting them to achieve their goals. And one of the pinnacles of this kind of achievement was his production of *Waiting for Godot* with senior company members Alvin Epstein and Jeremy Geidt—where he helped them to evoke the old age of the world.

In short, there is red state behavior and blue state behavior in the theatre, just as there is throughout the fifty states. Bumptious Tea Partyers could have learned a lot about generosity, humanity, and fraternity from watching David work with actors he loved.

Chief among the many other works of art that he helped develop, perhaps the most important, was his family, for David's achievements were not only artistic but domestic. I am speaking first of his beloved wife, Bronya, herself a powerful actor, of whom I still have vivid memories as the Nurse, in my production of Strindberg's *The Father*, putting a straitjacket on the unwitting Christopher Lloyd. And I am also speaking of his gifted, loyal, and devoted son, Lewis, so incredibly caring to his father during the last months of his life. I had occasion, recently, to see Lewis play the part of Jamie Tyrone in *A Long Day's Journey into Night* at The New Rep, and I thought: what a leap for an actor who so loved his father to play a character so alienated from his own. And I also thought: what a joy it must have been for David to have created such a sweet and talented legacy.

(2013)

Stanley Kauffmann

I became theatre critic for *The New Republic* in 1959, a year after Stanley Kauffmann began his more than half-century reign as that magazine's celebrated film critic. Born ten years after Stanley, I always felt like a younger brother, following in larger footsteps. His career covered almost every professional corner. After stints as an actor, playwright, and novelist, he then became an editor at Alfred Knopf (where he offered to publish my first book, an offer turned down by an agent, without consultation, who found the advance too low). When *The New York Times* offered me a job as its drama critic in 1966, I suggested it go to Stanley, who lasted about eight months and probably never forgave me. Having become Dean of the Yale Drama School soon after, one of my earliest acts was to invite Stanley to teach in the criticism department, along with Richard Gilman, where he attracted a host of brilliant students—Michael Feingold, David Copelin, Rocco Landesman, Jonathan Marks, Robert Marx, Roger Copeland, Francis Levy, Barbara Mackay, Jonathan Kalb, Jeremy McCarter, and scores of others.

Married for almost seventy years to his inseparable partner, Laura, Stanley was childless, but he had more loving and gifted kids than the old woman who lived in a shoe. Soon after coming to Yale, Stanley took over Gilman's place as theatre critic at *The New Republic* when Gilman moved to *Newsweek*, Stanley being the only writer I know to have covered film and theatre simultaneously for a single periodical. Those writings are preserved in a large number of published memoirs, film criticism, and theatre criticism, where he does battle with Andrew Sarris over the auteur theory and with Pauline Kael over whether to call a cinema product a film or a movie and whether *The Godfather* was a "movie" masterpiece or an overrated "film."

Those battles long over, how does one celebrate this protean man? One possibility is to remember that he was also one of the sweetest human beings ever to have lived on this planet. To be in the presence of Stanley Kauffmann, even when later he had become bed- and chair-ridden and increasingly deaf, was to be bathed in an aura of tenderness that his strong aquiline nose and penetrating eyes could not conceal. Over the years, and after the death of his beloved Laura, that 15th Street apartment became a kind of ashram for those who wished to absorb the wisdom and humanity of a truly generous spirit. Jeremy McCarter told me he would do anything in reading aloud this tribute for me except sing. Yet, you can sing the praises of Stanley Kauffmann without music, because the man was music itself of a kind that will always reverberate in our ears.

(2014)

Jeremy Geidt

The photos on my wall leap out at me as vivid invocations of the late, great actor and teacher Jeremy Geidt. His rotund, sometimes bearded features and mischievous eyes are gazing toward a host of fellow players over a period of almost fifty years. When I first met Jeremy, in 1965, he was a member of Peter Cook's touring Establishment Company, a satiric English troupe following in the footsteps of *Beyond the Fringe*. Learning the next year that he and his Arkansas-born wife, Jan, were eager to find an artistic home in America, I invited Jeremy to teach and Jan to administer at the Yale School of Drama, where I had just been appointed Dean and where he could get a chance to act with the newly formed Yale Repertory Theatre.

Apart from the fact that he never quite lost his Regent Street accent, Jeremy was the perfect model for our budding American resident company. He had trained for classical theatre with Michel Saint-Denis at the Old Vic School and later spent a few seasons with The Old Vic Company. As a result, he was comfortable in a wide range of roles and styles, in productions as diverse as the late David Wheeler's *Waiting for Godot* (opposite Alvin Epstein), where he played Gogo, and five Wheeler-directed Shaw plays, where he played all the patriarchs (mostly opposite Cherry Jones). He was in Ron Daniel's *Henriad*, where he played Falstaff, and Robert Wilson's *the CIVIL warS* and my Pirandello trilogy: *Right*

You Are, Six Characters in Search of an Author, and *Tonight We Improvise*. At the same time, during all those years, he was teaching a mask class, which floated on the obscene air of bawdy improvisations, as well as, later, a Harvard undergraduate course in Shakespeare, which won prizes every year.

He responded to any role, to any director, to any play, with the same bubbling enthusiasm a young actor might show toward his or her first stage opportunity. And this was a man who knew how to transform from character to character. One of the hazards of company work is that audiences may tire of your face. It never tired of looking at Jeremy's because it was rarely the same. He loved to work with actors who were also capable of this kind of transformation. The photos on my wall show him ogling Cherry Jones's Regina lubriciously through a window as Engstrand in *Ghosts*; as Osip, cynical servant of Mark Linn-Baker's Khlestakov, in a production of *The Inspector General* (Harvard senior Peter Sellars's first professional outing); playing Pantalone in two Gozzi plays, *The King Stag* (directed by Andrei Șerban with costumes, masks, and puppetry by Julie Taymor) and also *The Serpent Woman*, once again opposite Cherry Jones; downing a bottle of beer as Falstaff as he and Bill Camp—playing Hal—lounge lazily in front of a TV set; growling as the Old Shepherd in *The Winter's Tale* opposite John Douglas Thompson and Karen Macdonald; sitting languorously outside a sumptuous summer house as Gaev, brother to Claire Bloom's Ranevskya in *The Cherry Orchard*; as Peter Quince, rehearsing with Pyramus (Chuck Levin) and Thisbe (Joe Grifasi) in a forest where Carmen de Lavallade's Titania and Christopher Lloyd's Oberon crawl down Anthony Straiges's wooden scoop in Alvin Epstein's production of *A Midsummer Night's Dream* (then stage managing the skit, before a court audience that includes Meryl Streep as Helena); trying to tame a bumptious relative (Tony Shalhoub) in Diderot's *Rameau's Nephew*, under the direction of Andrei Belgrader; identifying Yorick's skull as the Gravedigger in *Hamlet* for Mark Rylance's melancholy Prince while digging the grave of Ophelia, played by Stephanie Roth; then, in repertory, soothing Mark Rylance's Treplev as Sorin in *The Seagull*; tending to a dying Chekhov (Jeremiah Kissel) as the German Dr. Schworrer in my *Chekhov on Ice*; mocking Will Lebow's Shylock as Salerio; and chastening F. Murray Abraham's King Lear as Kent.

This is just a sampling of the over one hundred and fifty roles that Jeremy played with the Yale Repertory Theatre and, later, when we moved to Harvard, with the American Repertory Theatre in Cambridge. He wouldn't want me to leave anybody out, but a full cast list would require three times as much space and time as I can inflict on grieving family and friends. I will only mention as a staggering fact that he spent over forty-seven seasons with the YRT and ART companies, the only even distant competition being Tommy Derrah (thirty), Alvin Epstein (twenty-seven), Karen Macdonald (twenty-five), Cherry Jones (thirteen), Will Lebow (thirteen), Remo Airaldi (eleven), and Tony Shalhoub (seven).

An ideal artist, mentor, and teacher, Jeremy was also the perfect pal—loyal and loving to an extreme. You could say these loyalties, in fact, affected his career. Totally devoted to the company ideal, he consistently rejected more lucrative acting offers from New York and Hollywood in order to remain with the resident company and fulfill his obligations to students, both at the college and the Institute. And I never heard him once say he regretted it.

What he valued more than the fame or money was advancing his art and that of other people dedicated to the same cause. He delighted in seeing some of the students he had trained at Yale (Tony Shalhoub, Tommy Derrah, Mark Linn-Baker, Kenneth Ryan, Harry Murphy, Eric Ellice, Steve Rowe, Rob Dean, Richard Grusin, Elizabeth Norment,

Marianne Owen) go on to join him as founding members of the ART company, just as he delighted in the success of his other students and associates—Meryl Streep—Sigourney Weaver—Christopher Durang—James Naughton—Christine Estabrook—Henry Winkler—Steve Zahn—Lewis Black—Dean Norris—Amy Brenneman, among them—if they found success in the world of Broadway, television or film.

But Jeremy was rooted. He loved the home on Garden Street that he shared for thirty-four years with Jan and his warmhearted, devoted daughters, Sophie and Jennifer. When they bought it in 1979, Jan and Jeremy worried that it would be too small. But anyone who visited them found the place so crammed with books, photos, paintings, posters, reviews, and dogs that it seemed as vast as the lobby of a theatre.

It was often crammed with people, too, the actors I've been celebrating, most of them here tonight. Some are too grief stricken to talk and have asked me to talk for them; some, like Claire Bloom and Jerry Kissel, send tearful regrets from other dressing rooms. As Jan prepared delectable victuals and generous drinks for hungry members of this loving family, the talk would get more and more thunderous, bibulous, and obscene. Being with Jeremy was like having a drink at the Mermaid Tavern before or after a show. He had bawdy names for everyone. (I called him Fartola; he called me Fartissimo.) I hope the Mermaid is one of your destinations, old heart. But you will be sorely, sorely missed at your Cambridge stomping grounds. Everyone who values theatre and actors and larger-than-life characters deserves a taste of your wit, a dose of your ribaldry, a touch of your loving spirit.

(2013)

Epilogue

"No epilogue, I pray you. . . . Never excuse; for when the players are all dead, there need none to be blame." The Duke's admonitory words to Peter Quince in A *Midsummer Night's Dream* have a particular poignance for me since Quince's part in our productions of *Midsummer* was always performed by Jeremy Geidt. But not all the players are dead yet, and there is at least one of them (me) left to be blamed.

One reason to blame me is that I have imposed such wintry views on such a comparatively young readership. (You, like virtually everybody else I meet these days, are no doubt younger than myself.) Another is that I may be claiming unity for such a disparate collection of pieces, written over different periods of time for different reasons and on different occasions. Yet, as I read over these articles while preparing them for publication, I do think I perceived a common purpose running through them, and that purpose is my desire to celebrate talent after a lifetime devoted to training it and prodding it onto roads less travelled by. This is, I suppose, a way of celebrating myself as well, since all teachers survive through the success of their students, and particularly through the kind of success they pursue. For it is through the quality and purpose of its artists that a nation partly defines itself. And it is through the strivings and achievements of its culture that a nation ensures an honorable future.

Index

like generation, 56-59
love generation (in 1960s and '70s), 56
masterpieces, 19-25
musical artists and Broadway musical, 25-35
return of Booboisie, 59-60
succession, 17
Wilder, Thornton Niven, 36-47
Cultural Revolution, 66
Curse of the Starving Class, 108

D

The Dance and the Railroad, 62
Daniels, Ron, 22
Danish Odin Teatret company, 62
The Death of Doctor Browne, 90
De Bris, Roger, 55
Defender of the Faith, 139
De Lavallade, Carmen, 134-135. *See also* Commemorative passages
Dickens, Charles, 42
Dionysus in 69, 23
Director, 15, 16
Broadway's, 46
Doctor skit, 51
Drama School, 4, 5
Dramatists, left-wing, 28
Duck Soup, 52
Durang, Christopher, 136-138. *See also* Commemorative passages
childhood years of, 136
satirizing sadistic nuns, 138
Dying, 65

E

Echoing, 66
Ego of theatre artists, 9
Egotism, 64
The Eighth Day, 39
Eliot, T.S., 137
Elitism, xiii
Elizabethan university wit, 112
Elizabethan World Picture, 105
Elliot Norton Award, 125
Elon, Amos, 102
Endgame, 21-22, 77
English comedy, 84

English period, 108, 109
Enrico IV, 97
Epstein, Alvin, 22, 135
The Eumenides, 70
Eureka Theatre, California, 132
Eustis, Oskar, 18, 131-134. *See also* Commemorative passages
Expressionism, 65
Eyes Wide Shut, 103

F

The Family Reunion, 70
Faulkner, William, 40
Federal Theatre, 93
Female employees, day care for, 10
Fichandler, Zelda, 17
The Fifth Column, 46
Fitzgerald, F. Scott, 45
Florence, 86
Founding Fathers, 3
42nd Street, 54
The Fountainhead, 13
Fragments of a Trilogy, 22
Frayn, Michael, 76
Freud, Sigmund, 98
Friel, Brian, 99
Fuegi, John (Brecht biographer), 28

G

Geidt, Jeremy, 146-149. *See also* Commemorative passages
Gelbart, Larry, 103
Gender bias, in American theatre, 99
German dramatists, 113
Gershwin, George, 28
Gersten-Vassilaros, Alexandra, 99
Ghia, Carmen, 55
Giamatti, A. Bartlett, 13
Gilbert, W.S., 83-86. *See also* Playwright passages
Gilbert and Sullivan in an Hour, 85
Glaspell, Susan, 100
Godot, 78
The Gondoliers, 85
The Goodbye Girl, 125
Gozzi's *King Stag*, 15
Grand (theatre in China), 60
The Great Gatsby, 109